*Praise for*

# Living the

# 80/20

# Way

*"Highly practical and full of examples ...The trick is to apply 'less is more' and 'more with less' to ourselves, our work and our relationships. This volume does not urge the reader to do more - measuring, managing, talking or whatever - but to do less in total by doing things differently. Koch suggests that once you make the breakthrough doing more with less 'is much easier than more with more.'"*

**The Independent on Sunday**

# RICHARD KOCH

## *Living the* 80/20 Way

Work Less
Worry Less
Succeed More
Enjoy More

NICHOLAS BREALEY
PUBLISHING

LONDON

*To Matthew*

First published by
Nicholas Brealey Publishing in 2004
Reprinted in 2004

3–5 Spafield Street
Clerkenwell, London
EC1R 4QB, UK
Tel: +44 (0)20 7239 0360
*Fax: +44 (0)20 7239 0370*

100 City Hall Plaza, Suite 501
Boston
MA 02108, USA
Tel: (888) BREALEY
*Fax: (207) 846 5181*

http://www.nbrealey-books.com
www.the8020principle.com

ISBN 1-85788-331-4

**British Library Cataloguing in Publication Data**
A catalogue record for this book is available from the
British Library.

Printed in Finland by WS Bookwell.

# Contents

The 80/20 Way enables

## *anyone*

to get *extraordinary* results

**without** extraordinary effort.

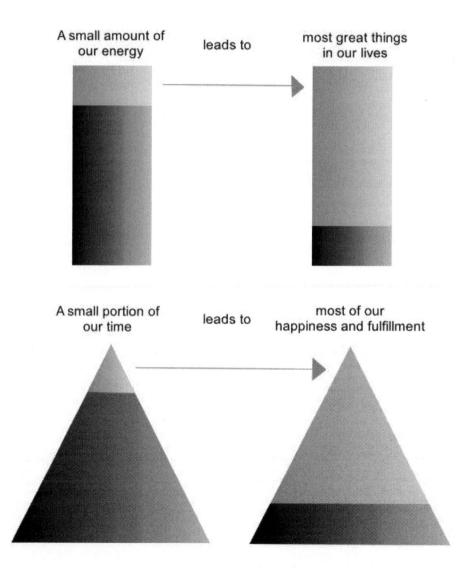

A small amount of our energy    leads to    most great things in our lives

A small portion of our time    leads to    most of our happiness and fulfillment

# *Preface*

If you knew you could always get more of the great things that life has to offer, with less effort and cost, would you be interested?

If you could work a two-day week and yet gain much better results and pay than you do for a full week now, would you be interested?

If you could find a simple solution to your problems by following a way that always works, would you be interested?

If this way applied not only to making a living, earning money, and finding success, but also to the even more important areas of life — the people you love and care for, as well as your happiness and fulfillment — would you be interested?

Of course you would. And you *can* transform your life if you follow the 80/20 Way.

The 80/20 Way involves a real change in how we see things and do things, yet following the 80/20 Way is simpler and easier than we have any right to expect.

How come? If we understand the way the world is really organized — even though that may be completely opposite to what we expect — we can fit in with that way and get much more of what we care about with much less energy. By doing *less*, we can enjoy and achieve *more*.

## This book is about action, but *less* action

This is an intensely practical book, but also a very unusual one, in that it is concerned with *less* action rather than more. As has been observed many times, it's impossible to make real improvements to our lives unless we *do things differently*. That's true — but the 80/20 Way also shows us how to *do less in total*. We do more of the things that make us happy, but since these are only a small proportion of everything we do, we can do fewer things in total and still transform our lives. We think more, do much more of a few things, and do them better and more intensely, but do much less overall.

## How I stumbled across the 80/20 Way

I can sing the praises of the 80/20 Way and say without hesitation how miraculous it is, because I did not invent it. The 80/20 Way is based on a scientific law called the 80/20 principle, which has been proven to work in business and economics. This says in essence that 80 percent of results come from only 20 percent of causes or effort.

*The 80/20 Principle*, my earlier book, explained how to use the concept to increase company profits. I also included a short section explaining how the 80/20 principle could work in our personal lives, to increase success and happiness. This application to individuals caused tremendous controversy. Some critics said that it was a perfectly respectable business idea but that it would never work outside business. Yet readers who tried it out wrote to say that the principle had changed their lives.

*The 80/20 Principle* has been translated into 22 languages and has sold well over half a million copies. Starting as a business book, published by business houses, and sitting on the business shelves in bookstores, somehow it has also become used and appreciated as a self-help book. The idea seemed to work so well that readers who tried it told their friends, and the friends who read the book told their friends, starting a word-of-mouth sensation.

Seven years later, I receive a steady and increasing stream of letters and emails from people everywhere around the world. Very few mention their business. They simply say what the Big Idea has done for their happiness and effectiveness: how it has helped them concentrate on the few relationships and issues that are really important to them, increased their sense of freedom, turbo-boosted their careers, and enabled them to escape the rat-race treadmill. Using the principle, they say, has taken away the guilt that used to make them waste their time, working so hard at things that were not important to them. The 80/20 principle has put them back in touch with who they are and what they really want out of their lives.

This is certainly true for me personally. The 80/20 principle helped me realize what is important for me. In 1990 I ditched a conventional career. I quit being a management consultant and started living fully again. I knew that I had to remain fulfilled, which would involve some "work," but I resolved that my life would drive my work and not the other way round. Since then, I've worked extensively on projects — writing books and being a "lazy entrepreneur," by which I mean creating new businesses but not doing any of the hard work myself — but only if they excited me.

With the exception of a year-long assignment in South Africa, I've not held a "proper job" since my decision and I've always allowed large tracts of time for family, friends, and sheer enjoyment of life. I have homes in London, Cape Town, and the sunniest part of Spain, and I take time to enjoy each place — often with very good friends staying — for several months a year. Yet I am *not* retired. By any objective standard, I'm achieving far more with an extremely relaxed lifestyle than I ever did when I worked all the hours God sent.

I'm utterly convinced that anyone can benefit hugely by working less and fulfilling their passions more. Rebalancing your life would not only create greater health and happiness, but probably also lead to far greater success — however you define that.

## GUIDE TO THE 80/20 BOOKS

*The 80/20 Principle*

❑ introduces the idea behind the 80/20 Way

❑ originally intended mainly for business readers

❑ how do I use the 80/20 principle to raise the profits of my corporation, and to be more effective personally?

*The 80/20 Individual*

❑ for managers and entrepreneurs

❑ how can I use the 80/20 principle professionally, to create wealth and wellbeing as an individual?

*The 80/20 Way*

❑ for everybody

❑ how can I use the 80/20 principle personally, to become happy and successful?

## Why this new book?

This book wouldn't have been written if it hadn't been for two people. First was Steve Gersowsky, a friend who runs a restaurant in Cape Town. Steve is bright and dynamic, full of life, and very savvy. I was taken aback when he said, "Tried to get into *The 80/20 Principle*. Found it too difficult. Couldn't get beyond page 10."

"You're kidding," I said.

"No really, man," he said, "all those numbers, professors, and statistics. All too much. Heard how great the book was, tried to get the hang of it, but I failed."

Then I realized that Steve hadn't failed; I'd failed Steve. I had thought that the book was breezy and easy. But I had to admit that although *some* of it, including most of the bits at the back helping individuals use the Big Idea, was easy to read, there were also illustrations about business that put off many non-business people. As the business section came first in the book, it gave the impression that the Big Idea was difficult, whereas in truth it is very simple.

As I was exploring for the first time in that book how to apply the 80/20 concept to our own lives, I threw ideas up in the air, leaving readers to work out how to catch and use them. I should have said, "That means we should do *this* to be happier."

An Australian friend, Laurence Toltz, also inspired the current book.

"The stuff you've written about is terrific," he emailed me, "but my dream is for people at all levels of income and education to be able to use it. Could you write a book to explain very simply how everyone can use the 80/20 principle to get round the problems they struggle with? *The 80/20 Principle* is written for business and professional people. Can you write a book for people not in business or without a tertiary education? A book to show them how to use the 80/20 Way for simple things like getting work they enjoy, or straightening out their finances?"

"Yes," I replied. "What a great idea! I'll start right away." And here it is.

## How does the 80/20 Way operate?

That's what the whole book is about! But I can explain what it's all about very briefly, because it revolves around two ideas:

- ❏   The law of focus: *less is more.*

- ❏   The law of progress: we can create *more with less.*

The idea of focus is easily understood. Chapter 1 will outline the concept that 80 percent of what we want is generated by 20 percent of what we do. Therefore when it comes to getting the results we want, to help the people and causes that are really important to us, only a very few things we do really matter. The rest are just a waste.

So if we learn to identify the things that matter most to us and add the greatest richness to our lives — if we learn to *focus* on the things we believe are most important — we discover that less is more. By concentrating on fewer things — the few really important aspects to our lives and the ones that work the way we want — life suddenly becomes deeper and more rewarding. This book will help you work out what truly matters to you and how to focus on these things.

The second idea — that we can *create more with less* — is not so obvious. The law of progress says that we can always obtain or accomplish *more* of what we want with *less* energy, sweat, and worry. This idea, that we can not only improve things dramatically but also do so with less effort, is so revolutionary, so contrary to conventional wisdom, that it's worth examining carefully.

This book shows you how to apply *less is more* and *more with less* to your self, work and success, money, relationships, and the simple, good life, and will help you develop a personal action plan to transform your life.

# PART I
## Introduction

# *What's the Big Idea?*

It is not necessary to do extraordinary things to get extraordinary results.

Warren Buffett

Modern life is a mistake. I'm not talking about the marvelous progress we have made in science, technology, and business, which has enabled us to eat better, stay younger, live longer, conquer disease, travel easily, and enjoy greater comfort than earlier generations.

It's the way we organize our personal and social lives that's a mistake. Instead of working to live, we live to work. If we had more self-confidence and the right philosophy, we could accomplish even more than we do now and enjoy our work more, yet labor for far fewer hours and conserve a larger part of our energy for our family and social lives.

This would be a major change in how we experience life. Here progress has run backwards. We used to enjoy more relaxed and balanced lives, with a more relaxed lifestyle, more free time, greater commitment to family and friends, greater social equality and fraternity, more civility to strangers, less stress and depression, less dependence on alcohol and drugs, and less addiction to money and power. We are now more conscious of ourselves and our individuality, but many of us are terrified of our new freedom. We worry far more, desperately seeking the illusion of security, which, despite our increasingly frantic striving, recedes ever further from us.

Life today divides into the fast track or the slow track. Both are less agreeable than the broad track of yesteryear. For many the slow track means economic insecurity: low earnings, low social standing, anxiety about unemployment, and missing out on the increasing material delights enjoyed by those on the fast track. But the fast track is not without its hazards. For many it means a single-minded obsession with getting ahead, total commitment to the job at the expense of personal relationships, and a frenzied lifestyle where work takes precedence over everything else. The fast track, too, brings anxiety and poverty, though in this case it's poverty of time and love rather than money.

If this analysis of the material advantages and personal disadvantages of modern life strikes a chord, I've great news. If we accept that modern life works at the material, scientific, and technological level, but often screws up our personal lives, I can announce that there's a novel way out of this box.

I am referring to the 80/20 principle, the observation that roughly 80 percent of results stem from 20 percent or fewer of causes. Later in this chapter I'll explain how the principle works and give many fresh examples. For the moment, let me just say that whereas the 80/20 principle has been used successfully in business and economics and has driven progress throughout the modern world, it has not yet been applied, on anything like the same scale, to the lives of individuals. If it *were* so applied, we could enjoy life much more, work less, and achieve more.

In reality, the best way to achieve *more* is to do *less*. *Less is more* when we concentrate on the few things that are truly important, not the least of which is happiness for ourselves and our loved ones.

What is this life, if full of care,

We have no *time* to
stand and stare.

*William Henry Davies*

I'll explain how and why using the 80/20 principle can cause a fundamental change in the way we approach life in Chapters 2 and 3. But I mustn't run ahead of myself. First, let me introduce you properly to the 80/20 principle, one of the most mind-blowing, far-reaching, and surprising discoveries of the past 200 years.

f we took 100 people and divided them into a team of 80 and a team of 20, we'd expect the team of 80 to achieve four times as much. And if we randomly selected the people, something like that would probably happen.

Yet imagine a **wonky** world,

where the 20 people achieve

# more results

than the other 80.

Make the wonky world even stranger. Imagine that not only do the 20 people achieve more than the 80, they achieve *four times more*.

This is exactly the wrong way round. We would expect the 80 people to achieve four times more than the 20. Now, in this curious and lopsided world, we imagine the reverse: the 20 people somehow manage to get four times the results of the other 80.

Impossible? Unlikely? Surely this wonky world, though not totally unthinkable, must be very rare.

What if one day we discovered that far from being unusual, the wonky world was actually *typical* — that the world *routinely* divides into a few very powerful influences and the mass of totally unimportant ones. Wouldn't this turn our whole view of life upside down?

*This is what happens when we discover the 80/20 principle.*

We find that the top 20 percent of people, natural forces, economic inputs, or any other causes we can measure *typically* lead to about 80 percent of results, outputs, or effects.

Counting the top cities in England, I found that the largest 53 cities had 25,793,036 people living in them, and next largest 210 cities or towns had 6,539,772. This is a terrifyingly precise 80/20 relationship: 20.2 percent of the cities have 79.8 percent of the people.[1]

It's worth spelling out the calculation:

❑     **53 out of 263 cities = 20.2%**

❑     **25,793,036 out of 32,332,808 people = 79.8%.**

The power of the 80/20 principle lies in the fact that it is *counter-intuitive*, it's not what we expect. We seem to be programmed — perhaps by our liberal culture or by an innate sense of fairness — to expect the picture shown in Figure 1, where causes and results are balanced roughly equally:

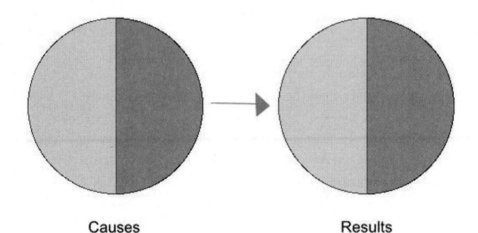

Causes                                           Results

**Figure 1  Causes and results: What we expect**

Instead, what we get is something totally different, more like Figure 2:

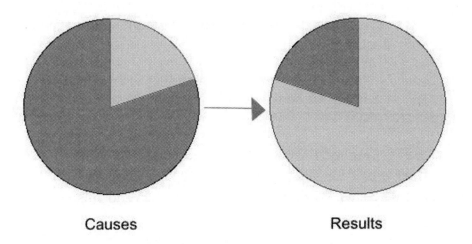

Causes                                    Results

Figure 2  Causes and results: What really happens

Here are some other illustrations:

❏      Five people sit down to play poker. It's likely that one of them
       — 20 percent — will walk away with at least 80 percent of the
       stakes.

❏      In any large retail store, 20 percent of the sales staff will make
       more than 80 percent of the dollar value of sales.

❏      Studies consistently show that 20 percent of customers lead
       to more than 80 percent of profits for any particular firm. For
       example, Toronto-based Royal Bank of Canada recently
       worked out how much profit each of its customers provided.
       It was staggered to learn that 17 percent of customers yielded
       93 percent of profits.

❏      Fewer than 20 percent of media stars hog more than 80 per-
       cent of the limelight, and more than 80 percent of books sold
       come from 20 percent of authors.

❏      More than 80 percent of scientific breakthroughs come from
       fewer than 20 percent of scientists. In every age, it is the

celebrated few scientists who make the vast majority of discoveries.

❏     Crime statistics repeatedly show that about 20 percent of thieves make off with 80 percent of the loot.

## WHO GETS THE MOST DATES IN SPEED DATING?

The latest craze for single people in New York and London — though it may have fizzled out by the time you read this — is speed dating.

It works like this. Put around 20–40 people in a room. The women sit down at tables and the men move from seat to seat. Each couple has between three and five minutes to talk before the man moves on to the next woman. Everyone has a unique number on a badge and you make a note of the number of anyone you'd like to go on a proper date with. The organizers collect the notes at the end of the evening and match up pairs who've liked each other. The next day they email the matches with names and contact details.

A major speed dating operator in the US confirms that most dates go to relatively few participants. "At least 75 percent of the interest goes to about 25 percent of the people," he comments. "Naturally they tend to be the most attractive people, but it's also true that about half of the guys who do well had been to speed dating before, and so were more confident about it."

It seems that to get a large number of dates, it's a good idea to attend at least two speed dating events.

Note that 80/20 is simply shorthand for a very lopsided relationship between causes and results. The numbers don't have to add up to 100. In some cases, 30 percent of causes may lead to 70 percent of results. Other examples may show a 70/20 relationship: 20 percent of causes lead to 70 percent of results. Or the split may be 80/10, or 90/10, or even 99/1.

We often find an even more exaggerated picture than 80/20 where far fewer than 20 percent of people or causes, in some cases as little as 1 percent or less, lead to at least 80 percent of results. Here are some very wonky cases:

❏ Betfair, the world's leading "betting exchange," where individuals take bets with other individuals, says that 90 percent of the money staked comes from 10 percent of its clients.

❏ In Indonesia in 1985, Chinese residents comprised less than 3 percent of the population, but owned 70 percent of the wealth.[2] Similarly, the Chinese are only a third of Malaysia's population, yet own 95 percent of its wealth.[3] In Mauritius, French families make up only 5 percent of the population but own 90 percent of the wealth.

❏ Out of 6,700 languages, 100 — the top 1.5 percent — are used by 90 percent of the world's people.

❏ In a famous experiment, psychologist Stanley Milgram randomly selected 160 citizens of Omaha, Nebraska and asked them to send a package to a Boston stockbroker, but not directly. They had to send the package to someone they knew personally, who then had to pass it on to another personal contact who they thought might know someone who knew someone close to the stockbroker, and so on. Most of the packages reached the stockbroker within six steps, leading to the idea of "six degrees of separation." But the point for us is that *more than half* the packages that made it to the stockbroker came through only *three* well-connected individuals in Boston. Those three people were more important, in getting the desired result, than all the other inhabitants of Boston.[4]

❏ Epidemics are caused by a tiny proportion of cases, which then have an effect out of all proportion to their numbers. For instance, in an outbreak of gonorrhea in Colorado Springs, neighborhoods comprising just 6 percent of the city's population accounted for 50 percent of cases. Investigation revealed that 168 people, who met in 6 bars, caused the whole epidemic. Less than 1 percent of the population of Colorado Springs was therefore responsible for 100 percent of the disease.[5]

❏ Americans comprise less than 5 per cent of the world's population, yet consume 50 percent of its cocaine.

❏ Much more than 80 percent of wealth created from new businesses comes from fewer than 20 percent of people who start them. Probably only 1 percent of new ventures in the past 30 years — including Microsoft, which is worth over $200 billion — account for 80 percent of the value created. Similarly, 1 percent of entrepreneurs — notably Bill Gates, who is worth more than $30 billion — make more than 80 percent of the money from new enterprises.

❏ Historical files reveal that police spies in Europe were aware of several thousand "professional revolutionaries" between 1847 and 1917. Yet only one of them — Vladimir Ilyich Ulyanov, who called himself Lenin — actually caused a lasting revolution. Thus 1 revolutionary out of more than 3,000 — 0.03 percent of revolutionaries — precipitated 100 percent of successful revolutions between those dates. Though this is an extreme example, history is full of cases where a tiny minority of players have diverted its whole course.

To be sure, the 20 percent or fewer of people who cause 80 percent or more of results — whether good or bad — are not randomly selected. They are not typical. They are interesting because they produce results that are at least 10 or 20 times greater than those produced by other people. As the high performers are not 10 or 20 times more intelligent than other people, it is the *methods and resources* they use that are unusually powerful.

## All of life

The 80/20 principle applies not only to groups of people and their behavior, but to virtually every aspect of life. There are always a small minority of very powerful forces and a great mass of unimportant ones. For instance:

❑   20 percent of countries, containing far fewer than 20 percent of the world's population, consume 70 percent of its energy, 75 percent of its metals, and 85 percent of its timber.

❑   Far less than 20 percent of the Earth's surface produces 80 percent of its mineral wealth.

❑   Fewer than 20 percent of species cause more than 80 percent of ecological degradation. It's estimated that just one species, out of the 30 million on earth — that's 0.00000003 percent — causes 40 percent of the harm. No prize for guessing the species.

❑   A very small percentage of meteorites falling to earth produce more than 80 percent of the damage.

❑   Far fewer than 20 percent of wars produce more than 80 percent of casualties.

❑   The overwhelming majority of baby seals in Alaska die young; 80 percent of the survivors come from 20 percent of the mothers.

❑   Wherever you go, fewer than 20 percent of clouds will produce 80 percent of rain.

❑   Less than 20 percent of all recorded music is played more than 80 percent of the time. If you go to a concert, whether rock or classical, the old familiar pieces — a tiny portion of the total repertoire available — will be churned out time and again.

❏ Fewer than 20 percent of the treasures in most art museums' inventories are on display more than 80 percent of the time.

❏ Of investments made by a successful venture capitalist, 5 percent of them provide 55 percent of cash, 10 percent produce 73 percent, and 15 percent yield a total of 82 percent.

❏ Fewer than 20 percent of inventions have more than 80 percent of impact on our lives. In the twentieth century, nuclear power and the computer probably had greater influence than the hundreds of thousands of other inventions and new technologies.

❏ More than 80 percent of food comes from far less than 20 percent of land. Also, fruit typically accounts for much less than 20 percent of the mass or weight of a tree or vine. And meat is a reduction of vast amounts of digested grain or grass.

❏ Drinks are also an extreme demonstration of the 80/20 principle. What makes Coca-Cola so much more valuable than any other soft drink on the planet? The sacred formula for tiny amounts of concentrate that, mixed with large volumes of water, produces "Coke." Or what produces beer and makes different beer brands distinctive? Minute proportions of hops and other flavorings.

❏ In fact, the whole process of life, from acorn to giant oak, from grain of wheat to a bread-bowl region, is the perfect expression of the 80/20 principle, taken to its fullest extent. Diminutive causes, massive results.

❏ Finally, evolution presents a stunning example of selectivity. One percent of species that have ever lived on earth, biologist Richard Dawkins estimates, constitute 100 percent of the species now living.

The 80/20 principle works everywhere in life. It's surprising and amazing. It's not what we expect. There is a big imbalance between causes and results.

# Most causes have little result,

## a few
### *transform life.*

**M**any people believe that the 80/20 principle, with its emphasis on the top 20 percent, is inherently elitist. But this is wrong. It is a fallacy that there is any restriction on who uses the 80/20 principle or that it is a zero-sum gain. It is not true that because I benefit from the principle, somebody else must lose.

To object to improvement on the grounds that it is elitist is wrong-headed: progress is desirable and helps everyone. Perfection and equality are equally impossible, and in my opinion equally undesirable. The 80/20 principle is no more elitist than, for example, money, private property, or vaccines against disease. Refusing to use any of these because they are "elitist" is silly. They are all tools that improve life for everybody.

Anybody can improve their life by using the 80/20 Way: the application of the 80/20 principle to our daily lives, with the objective of decreasing effort and worry and increasing happiness and the results we want. We use the 80/20 Way to go with the grain of the universe, producing better results more easily. When we do, other people benefit as well.

What would happen if *everybody* used the 80/20 Way? Everybody would be better off. Would there still be a top 20 percent and a bottom 80 percent of everything? Certainly. Unless there was, no further improvement would be possible. Only if we reached utopia or nirvana — a perfect world — would the 80/20 principle stop working.

Fortunately, that is not going to happen: we will always have something to improve.

As I know from my own experience, and as hundreds of thousands of people have discovered, using the 80/20 principle can have an enormous influence not just on our economy and society, but also on our personal lives. It can make us happy, fulfilled, and relaxed. We start by creating more with less...

# *Create More with Less*

Many might go to heaven with half the labor they go to hell.
Ben Jonson

All human history, all progress in civilization, involves getting *more with less.*

Nearly 8,000 years ago, humans moved from hunting savage animals and gathering wild fruits to a system of agriculture, cultivating land, and domesticating animals. Our ancestors got much more and better food with much less struggle and danger.

Until 300 years ago, 98 percent of the working population labored on the land. Then a new agricultural revolution used machinery to transform productivity. Today in developed countries, agriculture employs only 2–3 percent of the workforce, yet produces vastly more food, which is also more varied and nutritious. That's more with less.

The highway of economic progress in the past 400 years has also been more with less: identifying the few very productive forces and methods (the 20 percent) and multiplying them, so that more results can be obtained from fewer resources. Smaller and smaller amounts of land, capital, labor, management, materials, and time have been used to generate larger and better outputs: more steel for less iron ore, capital, and labor; more and better cars for less energy and cost; more consumer goods of every type, with more features and higher quality, at ever lower prices.

A century ago, computers didn't exist. Just 40 years ago, a few massive, clunky computers were made with enormous effort and cost. The planet's total computer power then was far less than that of the small laptop I'm using now. Computers keep getting cheaper, smaller, easier to use, and more powerful. They exemplify more with less.

Every material advance of humanity — in science, in technology, in living standards, in housing, in food, in health and long life, in leisure, in transport, in everything that makes modern life so much richer and more fun than before — gives more with less.

We can often get more with less simply by leaving something out. Algebra does this: it lets us compute more easily by *leaving out the numbers*, the basis for all computer programming breakthroughs. The World Wide Web operates by taking distance and location out of the equation. The Sony Walkman, a brilliant innovation, is really a cassette player minus the amplifier and speakers, yet it creates a fantastically versatile way of listening to music anywhere. A dry martini makes a great drink by cutting out the Martini.[1] The whole fast-food industry is simply restaurants without the waiters.

It is scant exaggeration to say that more with less is the basic principle by which modern science, technology, and business advance living standards everywhere.

The 80/20 principle says that a small minority of causes lead to a large majority of results. If we know what results we want, therefore, we can look for a super-productive way to get those results. The 80/20 principle guarantees that there is always a way. Every time, more with less is possible, provided that we identify the golden 20 percent: the people, methods, and resources that are extremely creative and productive.

Companies and countries that devise ways to deliver more value for less effort, peoplepower, and money flourish; but they can never rest on their laurels, because there is always a way to deliver even more for even less and somebody will soon find it. Because of the 80/20 principle, economic progress cannot stop.

## We don't apply more with less to our individual lives

Though the modern world has embraced the law of progress — the economic and scientific principle of more with less — it has consistently failed to apply the very same principle to the way we organize our private and social lives. The modern principle for individuals is *more with more*. To get more money, more status, a more interesting job, an exciting life, it seems to be necessary to give more and more to one's profession, job, company, or customers, sometimes to the point where there's no time or energy left for oneself, one's family, or one's friends, let alone for healthy relaxation or to recharge creative batteries.

Life in the fast lane turns into work in the fast lane. There is certainly more challenge, more stimulation, and more money, but there is also total submission to work demands, more burnout, and pervasive anxiety.

# How come we successfully use

## more with less

for *science, technology, and business*,

### and yet insist on more with more

## when it comes to our *working lives?*

If more with less works for companies and economies, it should work for individuals as well. In fact I know it does, from personal experience and from seeing many friends and acquaintances getting more with less: more satisfaction, more achievement, more money, more happiness, better relationships, and a more balanced and relaxed life, from less blood, toil, tears, and sweat.

Many of the things we do absorb energy but are worse than useless. Worry is a prime example. Worry is *never* useful. When we find ourselves worrying, we should either act and not worry, or decide not to act and not worry. If we can act to avoid a bad fate or reduce its chance of happening — and the action is worthwhile — then we should act and not worry. If, on the other hand, we can't control or influence what will happen, then worrying will cause us distress but not help us: we should not act and not worry. Worries will always arise but we can do without them, instantly deciding to act or not act, but in either case not to worry.

We have a big project ahead of us: nothing less than the reversal of modern work and living habits, the change from *more with more* to *more with less* in our personal, social, and professional lives.

It will take time. Social fashions don't change all that easily or quickly. The Calvinist notion that toil and trouble are essential for personal advancement is so deeply rooted in the culture and working assumptions of modern life that it will take a generation to uproot it. Yet the beauty of the 80/20 Way for any individual — for you and for me — is that we don't have to wait. We can start using it and benefiting right away.

## How to get more happiness with less effort

More with less is a practical tool that delivers on two promises:

- ❑ It is always possible to improve anything in our lives, not by a small amount, but by a large amount.

- ❑ The way to make the improvement is to ask, "What will give me a much better result for much less energy?"

It's not enough to seek improvement by means of greater effort or the same effort as today. A much better outcome must be sought *alongside lower effort*.

To expect more with less may seem unreasonable, but this is precisely the reason that amazing improvement is possible. The trap in making more effort to improve things is that we continue making the same kind of effort. We may improve things, but it will be a minor improvement and sooner or later we'll exhaust ourselves in the process. Instead, it should be plain that in making the startling demand for more with less, we are going to have to dream up a great breakthrough. By deliberately cutting back on what we put into the task and yet asking for much more, we force ourselves to think hard and do something different. This is the root of all progress.

Thinking hard may sound a bit frightening, but isn't it much better to do a little hard thinking, arrive at a much better result, and avoid a lot of hard doing? With a bit of practice, thinking how to get more with less becomes fun. The trick is to pick activities offering a higher reward for less energy.

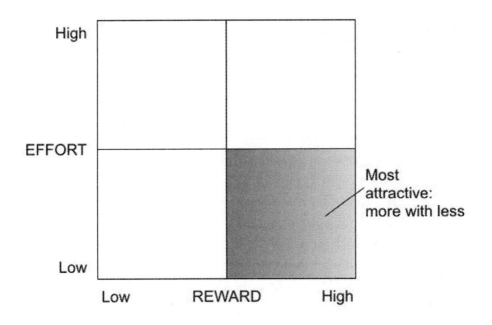

Figure 3  The more with less chart

Imagine you're a caveperson in the town of Bedrock, home town of *The Flintstones*. You need to get to the other side of town in a hurry. Your alternatives are to walk or run. Walking will take forever. Running is quicker, but more effort.

To run would be to make the very modern blunder of seeking more with more. It's the classic trap of trying to secure a better result by working harder.

The 80/20 Way is different. We demand, quite unreasonably, a much better result with much less effort. But since we know that more with less is possible, we continue thinking until we have a more with less solution. How can we get across Bedrock much faster but without the slog of running?

Like the waitress at the prehistoric diner, we could rollerskate with less energy than it would take to run, yet arrive quicker. Or we could go one step further and jump on the back of a friendly brontosaurus. That's more with less.

Or imagine that you're a teenager wanting a date with an attractive boy or girl. The more with less chart might look like Figure 4.

You can think about how nice the date would be, but do nothing. Easy but useless.

You could draw attention to yourself, maybe becoming president of the debating society or winning an athletics event. But the boy or girl you are after may not notice or care — a high-effort, low-reward approach.

You could spend ages trying to win over his or her parents, hoping that they'll arrange a date. This may work, but only with extraordinary effort.

Or you could simply go up the object of your desire, put on your best genuine smile, and ask for a date — easy and just as likely to work.

This example is obvious, but you can draw a more with less chart for anything in your life. With a little imagination, you'll come up with a higher-reward solution that uses less energy.

I am *not* saying that we should take the path of least resistance or never dedicate ourselves 100 percent to an activity or cause that is dear to us. The choice is ours. If we go for the right activities, we can work effortlessly and achieve a great deal, or we can put everything into what we do and achieve even more.

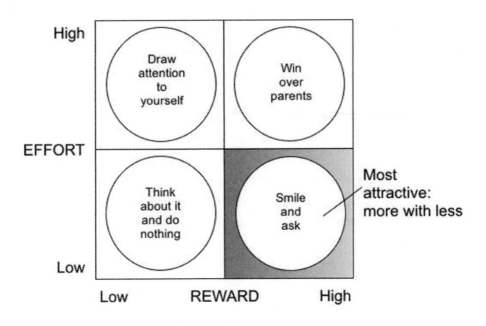

Figure 4 Teenager wanting a date

Think of any great scientist, musician, artist, thinker, philanthropist, or business leader.

- ❏ Do they achieve by trying to do something they find easy and natural, or by trying to do something that is hard and unnatural?

- ❏ Do they achieve because they work hard, or because they find it easier than other people to excel in their chosen arena?

- ❏ Do they work hard because they feel guilty, or because they identify with their work, believe in it, and love it?

Even when they work hard, their work is always economical — they get a huge return on their effort.

In our personal lives, there are always things we can do that work very well, yet take little money or effort. It's incredibly corny, but the best things in life *are* free or nearly free, giving a fantastic return on effort.

Saying thanks, showing appreciation, displaying affection, watching a sunrise or sunset, caring for a pet or a plant, smiling at a casual acquaintance or stranger, committing a random act of kindness, enjoying a walk in a beautiful place — these are all ways of getting more with less. The reward is out of proportion to the effort.

If you think about it, the only way to take leaps forward in our lives is to demand more with less. The beauty of more with less is that it can be applied to anything, it always works, and it always gives an answer you can keep up throughout your life. The problem with more with more is that it's not sustainable. More with less is easy to maintain and extend. A bit of upfront thinking is a small price for a huge lifetime reward.


## What's difficult becomes easy

One final element of more with less that can make a big difference to our lives is the role that habit plays. Anything we do is much more difficult the first time, and gets progressively easier the more we do it, to the point where it becomes easier to do it than not to do it. A terrific example is exercise. Walking five miles is extremely tough the first time you do it, but if you do it every day, nothing could be easier. In fact, both body and mind get used to anything we do after about two weeks: it becomes second nature.

What's difficult becomes

# easy

and what's easy

often creates *difficulties*.

Although we can change our habits at any time, it's easier to change earlier in life. If we always do what's easy — such as overeating, driving everywhere rather than walking, or getting angry at the least provocation — we'll find it difficult to reverse the habit a few years later. On the other hand, if we do a *few hugely worthwhile* things that are hard to start with, we'll find before long that they become easy.

A few great habits are vital because without continuous renewal we can lose things we've worked very hard for. It doesn't matter, for example, how intense a fitness program is — after a month of inactivity all the benefits will be gone. Why work hard for nothing, when a few habits that become second nature can give you a healthy rhythm every day?

We get more reward with less energy if we adopt rewarding habits earlier rather than later. But also, given human nature, we'd better be *selective* about the good habits we're going to adopt. We get more happiness with less effort if we carefully select a few excellent habits we'd like to have and master these, not bothering about all the other good habits we could in theory cultivate. There's a limit to the number of good habits most of us can practice. Yet a few habits can have a phenomenal effect on our happiness throughout life — we get a massive bonanza from a little upfront effort.

It's for you, not me, to decide which high-payoff new habits to cultivate now (you'll lose out by leaving it till later). You shouldn't choose a habit because it's morally "good," but because of the huge benefit to you. Just choose seven super-rewarding habits that will be your friends for life.

Overleaf are some examples of habits with huge benefits (if the benefits matter to you; only you can judge). Choose your seven high-payoff habits carefully! Get more happiness for less effort!

## EXAMPLES OF HIGH LIFETIME PAYOFF HABITS[2]

| Habit | Payoff |
|---|---|
| Daily exercise | Much better health, more attractive body, feeling great |
| Daily intellectual exercise | Keep alert, increase intelligence, enjoy thinking |
| Doing one altruistic act a day | Makes you happy |
| Meditating or quiet thinking each day | Clear mental clutter, make better decisions |
| Daily nurturing of your lover | Keep him or her; make them happy |
| Always give praise or thanks where possible | Makes other person *and you* feel good |
| Save and invest 10 percent of income | A future free of money worries |
| Being generous to friends | Deepen relationship, feel good |
| Always having 2–3 hours of pure relaxation every day[3] | Renew your energy, keep happy and healthy |
| Never lying | Evokes trust, enhances reputation |
| Keeping calm and relaxed always | Feel good, better health, longer life |
| Focusing on what matters to you | Making more out of less |
| Deciding *never* to worry: always to *act and not worry* or *not act and not worry* | Peace of mind, reduction of effort |
| Habitually asking yourself how to get *more with less* | Dramatic improvement to any situation |

Pick the few high-payoff habits that will make *you* happiest. The list is far from exhaustive, so add any habits that have the potential to make you very happy, then master your seven.

## More with less: The final frontier

What's most precious to us and in short supply? What will we be most upset to see run out?

The answer is probably *time.*

It might seem unbelievable that more with less applies to the thing we think we're shortest of in life: time. Yet however strange it seems, that claim is true...

# We Have All the Time in the World

Time is a gentle god.

Sophocles

At the age of 30, an extremely successful Wall Street trader decided to go to Tibet, enter a monastery, and undertake rigorous spiritual studies.

On his first day, while his fellow trainees were hanging back, the ex-trader marched up to the top Zen master and asked, "How long does it normally take to become enlightened?"

"Seven years," the Zen master replied.

"But I was top of my class at Harvard Business School, I made $10 million at Goldman Sachs, and in preparation for entering the monastery I've taken all the best time-management courses. How long will it take me if I study intensively and try extremely hard to cut the time?"

The Zen master smiled and said, "Fourteen years."

On the other hand, do you remember the story about Archimedes? He was having a quiet bath one day, slopped some water over the side, then suddenly leapt in delight from his tub and ran naked through the main street of Athens, shouting at the top of his lungs, "Eureka! I've got it!"

He'd discovered an important theory. It took just a moment of inspiration, while he was relaxing, thinking about nothing much.

Time is like that: cussed when we try to speed up, a dear friend when we slow down.

hat's this got to do with the 80/20 principle? Time is perhaps the best example of the principle, and the one of most value to our lives. If we create high value at work, we'll achieve at least 80 percent of it in 20 percent of our time. In our personal lives, we'll attain 80 percent of our happiness and value to those we love in 20 percent or less of our time.

Once we realize this, our lives are transformed. Suddenly, there is no shortage of time. There is no rush. If we think intelligently about what we can achieve with our time, we can be relaxed, even lazy. In fact, being lazy — having plenty of time to think — may actually be a precondition for achieving a great deal.

This was true for the ancient Greeks. With slaves to do all the work, they spent their time thinking, debating, and in leisure pursuits. Result: the greatest civilization, science, and literature that had ever existed. It is also true of developed modern society. Because most of us don't have to labor with our hands, we use our minds to create great wealth, science, and culture.

Yet here is a paradox. We have never been so free, yet failed to realize the extent of our freedom. We have never had so much time, yet felt we had so little. Modern life bullies us to speed up our lives. We use technology to do everything faster. But in racing against the clock, all we do is stress ourselves out. Going faster doesn't give us more time — it makes us feel that we're always behind. We battle against time, our imagined enemy. We perceive time as accelerating, draining out from our lives at an alarming rate.

Andrew Marvell wrote:
"But at my back, I always hear

Time's wingèd chariot, hurrying near."

Henry Austin Dobson wryly observed:
"Time goes, you say? Ah no!

Alas, Time stays, we go."

However, Marvell, Dobson, and modern life are all wrong. We can have more with less: more happiness with less time, more results with less time.

The 80/20 Way overturns the modern view of time, freeing us to enjoy our lives without worrying about time. Time is not in short supply, we are awash with it. Time need not rush, nor need we. Time can stand still, bringing us happiness, achievement, and a taste of eternity.

Time is a boundless sea. We can swim happily in time, confidently, calmly, with no sense of impending doom. Dear old Sophocles was right after all: Time is a gentle god.

There are two ways in which we experience time. There is the small quantity of time — the 20 percent or less — that delivers 80 percent of what we want. And there is the much larger quantity of time — the 80 percent or more — that delivers a miserable 20 percent.

Time doesn't run at a constant rate. Time flows in fits and starts, in gurgles and splurges, in trickles and floods. There are long periods when nothing happens, and short bursts when a tidal wave transforms our world. The art of time surfing is to track down the waves and ride them to happiness and success. Time is not absolute — time is relative to our emotions, our attention, and our timing.

There are times when we are totally absorbed, absolutely happy, in tune with the universe — when time stands still. We are scarcely conscious of time or ourselves. We are in the zone, in the moment, experiencing a sense of inner calm or bliss.

"Time *flew by*," we say.

"The day just

# di**S**appeared."

These are the rare moments when we feel happiest and when we achieve the most. A little like Archimedes, we may have a breakthrough insight or idea. We may make a decision that changes lives. These small fragments of time are worth many days, weeks, months, or years of "normal" time.

At other times, little worthwhile happens. We are bored, miserable, or unexcited. In these dog days, time doesn't race past or stand still, it drags heavily along.

Is time from the first category the same in character and value as time from the second category? Hardly. A day of time in the zone may be worth a lifetime of dog days. *Less is more.*

The value of time, and how we experience it, depends on on how we use it: how we feel about our lives — at the time.

- ❏ We are likely to experience 80 percent of our happiness in 20 percent of our time.

- ❏ 80 percent of our time may only contribute 20 percent of our happiness.

- ❏ Probably 80 percent of what we achieve comes from 20 percent of our time...

- ❏ ...and the other 80 percent of our time only leads to 20 percent of our achievement.

It follows that:

- ❏ Most of what we do is of limited value, for us and everyone else. French novelist La Bruyère wrote, "Those who make the worst use of time most complain of its shortness."

- ❏ A few things that we experience and do, in very little time, are of enormous value. We get a fantastic return on our time when 20 percent of time leads to 80 percent of happiness or achievement — we get a fourfold or 400 percent return on this time.

❑ If we only make good use of a small portion of our time, there can't be any great shortage of it. If 80 percent of our time leads to 20 percent of value to us, then the return on this time is only 20 divided by 80, or 25 percent. The issue is not time, but what we do with it. We can get a paltry 25 percent return on our time, or 400 percent.

❑ If we are self-employed and spend two days a week on our most valuable type of activity, we should be able to get 160 percent of the value that used to take five days to generate — and still have three days left over for whatever we want.

❑ We can sharply boost the quality of our lives by changing our use of time. If we do more of the few things that make us happy and productive, and much less of the many activities that take most of our time but don't lead to high levels of happiness or achievement, we can improve our lives in a sensational way — all with less effort!

❑ We normally experience "good" time, which is short, and "bad" time, which is long. What if we switch them? If we make the "good" time long and the "bad" time short, we revolutionize our lives.

Of course, happiness and personal effectiveness can't be measured precisely. The 80/20 numbers are approximate. Still, multiplying the value of our time by four — a good rule of thumb — is like living to be 320 instead of 80, without any of the disadvantages of old age!

## What are your happiness islands?

*Happiness islands* are the small dollops of time — the special, glorious times — when we're happiest.

Think back to the last time you were really happy, then the times before that.

What did these times, or some of them, have in common? Were you in a special place, with a particular person, or pursuing a similar sort of activity? Are there some common themes?

How can you *multiply* your time spent on happiness islands? If you figure out that your happiness islands make up 20 percent of your time, how could you take that to 40, 60, or 80 percent?

If 80 percent of your time leads to only 20 percent of your happiness, can you cut those activities, freeing up time for things that make you happy?

Luckily, there are always many activities that give us a poor return on happiness for the time spent. Surveys of people watching television, for example, show that very few say they are happy after watching hours of TV. Typically, they feel mildly depressed. If watching television makes you happy, do more of it; but otherwise, stop!

What other things that have a poor happiness return could you quit doing? What do you do out of a sense of duty? If there's little pleasure in the duty, how much good are you doing? If you were happy, your happiness would overflow into the lives of those around you. Time spent being miserable is antisocial.

Ask yourself,

### if most of my time

doesn't make me happy,

# how can I

spend *less time* on these activities?

## What are your achievement islands?

When they first hear about the 80/20 principle, many people get the wrong end of the stick. "The idea's all very well in theory," the head of a charity told me recently, "but I haven't been able to make it work in practice. I can't confine myself to the top 20 percent of what I do — real life doesn't allow that kind of pace to be maintained for long."

"What do you think your most valuable 20 percent is?" I asked.

"Well, rushing around giving speeches, raising money, meeting the great and the good. I can do two lunches and two dinners a week where I make speeches, but any more than that and I get burned out."

"But that's probably *not* your most valuable time," I countered. "Think about the small amounts of time when you have been relaxed and yet have achieved a great deal. Have you had any of those times recently? Maybe when you had a brilliant new idea?"

"Oh, I see what you mean. There was an afternoon which was so beautiful and I was worn out, so I went home and sat in a deckchair in the garden. I was goofing off, really, but then I had the idea for our new campaign. And it's true, we raised five times more from that campaign than the one a year ago."

*Achievement islands* are the small time periods when you are your most productive or creative: when you get more with less, accomplishing the most with little apparent effort in very little time. What are yours?

Do they have things in common? Do they happen at the same time of day? Are the activities similar, such as selling, writing, or making decisions? Do they happen in a special place, with particular colleagues, or after the same event or stimulation? What mood are you in? In a group or alone? Rushed or relaxed? Talking, listening, or thinking?

How could you multiply time on your achievement islands and reduce time on everything else?

Richard Adams was a bored, disillusioned, middle-level bureaucrat. When he was 50 he dreamt up a bedtime story for his daughter, Juliet, who loved rabbits. *Watership Down* sold over seven million copies, transforming Adams' life.

Could you spend more time on the things you enjoy, even without quitting your day job? Could a hobby, interest, or sideline in your life blossom into a new career? Find out: spend more time on the things you enjoy. Try out your new projects while you are still working at your normal job. Experiment with different ideas until one clicks.

## The poor daydreaming clerk

Once there was a wayward school kid. Expelled for being disruptive, he found a badly paid job as a junior clerical officer. He was so bored at work that he found plenty of time for daydreaming and reading about science. He fancied himself as a self-taught, amateur scientist.

The kid was Albert Einstein. In his mid-twenties he rocked the scientific world with the theory of relativity. He'd sussed it while at the Swiss patent office in Berne for the previous four years. He relished the rest of his life as the first "celebrity scientist."

Many great ideas have come from people doing ordinary jobs. Time that would otherwise be wasted and miserable can become hugely creative and enjoyable.

Think about the 80/20 questions overleaf. To answer them, try thinking about or writing down *everything that really excites you*, that you love doing in any part of life — at work, your hobbies and sports, the best minutes of each day. Then either choose one of these activities and make it central to your life, or work out what the activities have in common and do more of that, and less of everything else.

For example, my life took a turn for the better when I realized that what I loved doing was evoking enthusiasm: getting an individual, or more often a group, all geed up about a topic or cause that I myself felt strongly about. That is why I now spend most of my time writing books, giving speeches, and talking to friends about ideas that excite us all. There is no standard job category for evoking enthusiasm — and yet the insight that it's the thing I enjoy most and do best has led me to a fuller and richer life, while also doing less. I now have a simple decision rule: If

I'm asked to do something, and it doesn't involve evoking enthusiasm, I say no.

What's the equivalent for you?

---

## 80/20 QUESTIONS

❏ Could I enjoy life more by developing a personal interest or obsession that drives me? Might it lead to a new career?

❏ Could I take the small part of my time that most excites me and make a career out of it?

❏ What questions could I ask myself to jump-start my inspiration?

---

## Down with time management, up with time revolution

Don't try to "manage" your time.

You try to manage something if you are short of it; money, for example. But we are *not* short of time. We may be short of ideas, confidence, or common sense, but not time. What we *are* short of is those marvelous times when time stands still, when we are wonderfully happy and creative.

Time management tells us to speed up. It promises us more free time, time to relax, but it doesn't deliver. The promise is just a carrot to make us move faster. Like the donkey, we find ourselves moving faster but remain those few elusive inches away from the carrot. In today's faster world, hours are longer, work less leisurely, and pressure more intense. Like the donkey, we have been conned. With time management, we work more and relax less.

*Time revolution* says the opposite. We have too much time, not too little. It is because we have so much time that we squander it.

To detonate your time revolution, slow down. Stop worrying. Do fewer things.

**Chuck** your *to do list,*
make a

# not to do list.

Act less, think more. Reflect on what really matters to you. Stop doing anything that isn't valuable, that doesn't make you happy. Savor life.

The modern world has accelerated out of control. Technology was meant to add to our free time, but it's done the opposite. As Theodore Zeldin says:

> Technology has been a rapid heartbeat, compressing house-
> work, travel, entertainment, squeezing more and more into
> the allotted span. Nobody expected that it would create the
> feeling that life moves too fast.[1]

Swim against the tide of acceleration. Be unconventional, even eccentric. Purge your diary. Dump your cell phone. Stop going to meetings or events that bore you. Reclaim time for yourself and the people you care about.

## Time revolutionaries

Like many, I admire Warren Buffett, the investor who's the planet's second-richest person. I don't admire him for his business acumen or his money, but for his wildly unconventional way with time.

He runs America's biggest, richest conglomerate empire. But does he rush around? Is he super-busy? Absolutely not. He says he "tap dances to work." Once there, he "expects to lie on his back and paint the Sistine chapel ceiling." His style, he says, "borders on lethargy." He makes very few decisions, only the extremely important ones. By being relaxed and thoughtful, he usually gets them right.

Of people I've known, who gets my number one time revolutionary award? Step forward Bill Bain, the founder and former leader of a very successful management consulting firm.

I was a partner there for two years. Everyone worked long and hard — with one exception. I'd often run into Bill in the elevator. He was always dressed immaculately. Always entering or leaving the office, often in spot-less tennis gear. Bill made all the key decisions, and made a fortune, with very little time and effort.

Management consulting is hard labor. Yet "Jim," a friend and partner, also bucked the trend. We first worked together in a tiny, cramped office, full of noise and frenzied activity. Everyone dashed madly around. Except Jim. There he sat, calmly examining his calendar and languidly writing down his objectives. Our job was to execute them. Jim was wonderfully effective.

"Chris" was another consultant and time revolutionary. He sold multimillion-dollar assignments. The troops loved him. He was always in the office early in the morning and late at night. Yet his reputation for long hours was undeserved. Chris routinely spent afternoons discreetly playing golf or tennis, at the racetrack, or taking long lunches. Everyone assumed that he was with clients. When I once chided him, he said he was following the 80/20 Way, getting more results with much less energy. I had to agree it was true!

## Live in the present

The present moment is vital. Don't live in the past or the future. Don't worry about the past or the future. Get more with less — confine yourself to the present moment and enjoy concentrating on it.

Time doesn't run out. Nor does it run from left to right. As round clocks tell, time keeps coming round. Time enjoyed in the past is still there. Our achievements and good deeds still stand. The present is real and precious, regardless of how long or short our future will be. We can be proud of our past and we can hope for our future, but we can only live in the present.

The 80/20 view of time makes us more relaxed and "connected." Relaxed, because time gone is not time used up. We are more connected to what is going on now and to other people.

We have the precious gift of life today, to be enjoyed and experienced how we choose. Each moment of life has the quality of eternity, the stamp of our own individuality. When time stands still, we are totally absorbed in the present. We are everything and we are nothing. Time is fleeting and eternal. We are happy, life has meaning. We're part of time, and also outside it.

Time revolution brings us more joy in less time. When the present moment has meaning, time is one seamless whole, valuable yet inconspicuous. The rush is over, anxieties recede, bliss increases. We can be intensely happy in no time at all. When we are at one with life and the universe, we step outside time. We reach the highest form of more with less.

## Improving key elements of your life

It's time to move on to Part II, where we apply less is more and more with less to five key areas of life:

- ❏     Your self

- ❏     Work and success

- ❏     Money

- ❏     Relationships

- ❏     The simple, good life.

In each area we learn to focus, so that less is more. We'll also see how to improve life — dodging the strain and stress imposed by the more with more treadmill, learning to enjoy more with less.

The emphasis throughout is on practical action steps, and in Part III you and I will carry this to its final conclusion, developing a personal action plan enabling us to thrive in the modern world while elegantly side-stepping its wearisome woes.

# PART II
# *Making a Living and a Life*

# Focus on Your Best 20 Percent

> I've got more energy now than when I was younger because
> I know exactly what I want to do.
>
> legendary ballet master George Balanchine

When he was 12, Steven Spielberg decided to be a movie director. Five years later he visited Universal Studios. He ducked out of the standard tour to find a real movie being made. The 17-year-old buttonholed the head of Universal's editorial department to tell him about the films he was going to make.

Next day Spielberg dressed in a suit, loaded his dad's briefcase with two candy bars and a sandwich, and marched boldly through the gate into Universal Studios. He commandeered a deserted trailer, writing "Steven Spielberg, Director" on the door. He became a fixture on the lot, mixing with directors, producers, writers, and editors, sucking in ideas, observing how real directors behaved.

At the age of 20, Spielberg showed Universal a small movie he'd made and won a seven-year contract to direct a television series. Later, of course, he made a string of hits, including *ET*, one of the highest-grossing movies of all time.

Spielberg was focused.

Focus is the secret of all personal power, happiness, and success. Focus means doing less; being less. Focus makes less more. Few people focus, yet focus is easy. Focus expands individuality, the essence of being human.

## Who are you? Who do you want to become?

Life's greatest mystery is human character and uniqueness. We craft individuality. Other animals can't. We share 98 percent of our genes with chimpanzees, yet the 2 percent variation makes all the difference.

We're not totally subject to our genes. In creating stories, ideas, music, science, and popular culture, in thinking and communicating, humans do surprising things that our genes wouldn't.[1]

Our destiny lies in becoming individuals — creating and fulfilling our unique potential. We each evolve differently and unpredictably.

Individuality implies differentiation. *Becoming different requires editing, subtraction, focus.* We become dissimilar by focusing on our distinctive and authentic parts.

True, we're not blank slates. Our genes determine our appearance and have a big say in many other matters. As we grow up, our parents and family influence how we behave, think, and think of ourselves. Our teachers, friends, priests, bosses, and mentors mold us. The ideas and norms of our society, and the groups with whom we hang out, strongly sway us.

Yet subtract all these influences and there's still something left: the precious and strange thing called our *self*, our unique identity and autonomy. However pronounced the pressures on us, we have our own personality. Nobody else on the planet is the same. In a big or small way, we are bound to influence the world, making it different than it would be without us.

We become individuals though *subtraction*. Less is more.

We have the wonderful opportunity to let go of the bits of ourselves that are not authentic, not "really us" — the parts imposed by background, parents, and environment. The authentic self is a small part of our total self, yet it's the vital self. We all have special gifts, unique imaginations, our little bit of genius: the spark of life that's wholly ours.

When we focus our self, we give up doing what many other people do, thinking what others think. Is this a loss? Of quantity, yes; but not of quality. In quality, less is more. By narrowing our interests, we deepen and intensify them. By focusing on our best, unique attributes, we become more individual, more *human*. We focus our power, our singularity, and our ability to enjoy life profoundly and uniquely.

Developing individuality is a conscious process. It involves deciding who you are and who you are not; who you want to become and who you don't want to become. We become more distinctive individuals through deliberate decisions and actions, honing and increasing what is different and best about us.

## Focus and individuality make life easier

Many people meander through life, muddling along without great hope or direction. They think this is the easiest way. But is it? Are they short-changing themselves?

Developing one's authentic self, the vital and best part of oneself, is not difficult or unnatural. In being true to your self, you give up the parts of you that are not genuine or natural. You stop acting. You stop pretending to be interested or excited in things that bore you. You stop worrying about what other people think of you. What could be easier? More rewarding? What could electrify your life more?

The modern world overloads us. We try to keep up with so many things. We make zillions of little decisions. It's way too much. How much simpler to make a few big decisions!

As Amy Harris wryly observes, "Nuns do not need to keep up with *Vogue.*"

We can't honestly care intensely about too many people or too many things. We can't be devoted to many people or causes at once.

Life is easier after making a few big decisions:

❏     Who and what do you care most about?

❏     What kind of person are you and want to become?

❏     What are your strongest qualities, emotions, and abilities?

❑ Do you want to commit to one life partner? Who?

❑ Do you want to raise children?

❑ Do you want to make a name for yourself? For what?

❑ Do you want to work for yourself or on your own terms? At what?

❑ Do you want to create something that other people will notice and enjoy?

❑ Do you want to have a "cottage small by a waterfall"?

❑ What are you putting energy into that isn't essential for your happiness?

All of these decisions *exclude*. They simplify life, close off options, eliminate excess choice. They concentrate energy. What are you putting energy into? Is your personal power focused?

When trying to answer questions like these, don't be afraid to ask good friends or mentors for help. Use these people as a sounding board — most of us need assistance from others before we discover what is best for us.

Whether you believe you can do something

or you believe you can't,

*you're right.*

Focus decreases doubt and turbo-charges confidence and power. As Shakespeare wrote in *Measure for Measure*:

Our doubts are traitors,
And make us lose the good we oft might win,
By fearing to attempt.

We all have a tremendous, underused asset: our sub-conscious mind and emotions. The subconscious is a friendly and truly *personal* computer. It's always switched on, always churning away.

The subconscious can resolve dilemmas, breed brilliant ideas, bring us peace and joy. Like the personal computer itself, the subconscious delivers much more with much less energy and cost.

How many times have you been walking the dog, brushing your teeth, meditating, or sitting in a deckchair, when suddenly — Wham! Eureka! The conscious mind wasn't working on the issue. The subconscious was, delivering the answer you needed.

The subconscious is selective. When you care deeply about an issue, it takes note. It doesn't process weak or mixed messages. The subconscious works best when you're focused on one issue. Less is more.

## Focus and individuality make us happy

Happiness is not outside us. Happiness is inside. Our minds and our emotions, and what we think of ourselves, make us happy or unhappy. We are happy if we have high self-respect and self-esteem.

Self-esteem can be *temporarily* boosted by drugs or drink, flattery, power, money, or by deceiving ourselves. Yet the reliable, lasting way to high self-esteem is by nurturing the best of our selves. A positive and accurate self-image is based on individuality: an authentic sense of who we are and why we live life our way. Lasting happiness cannot be gained through consumption. Happiness requires active participation in what we value. To do things well, enjoy them, and take pride in what we have done — these fertilize happiness; they demand development and individuality.

Reaching for the best *only* in the areas that suit you is more fun than bother. Getting the best becomes relatively easy.

*It's a funny thing about life –*

if you refuse to accept anything but the best,

*you very often get it.*
*Somerset Maugham*

Creative emotions possess and delight us. They come from caring, attention, focus, consistent dreaming, from passionately wanting to create.

To dance well, love well, raise children well, play golf well, cook well, ask questions well, direct a movie well — inspired actions make us happy. Individuality and focus make us happy.

## The 80/20 Way to focus and improvement

Here's a three-step process to make dramatic improvements to any part of your life:

❏ Step 1: Focus on your 80/20 destination — *where you want to be.*

❏ Step 2: Find the 80/20 route — *the easiest way to the destination.*

❏ Step 3: Take 80/20 action — *the first key steps.*

## Step 1: Focus on your 80/20 destination

A destination is where you want to arrive *and* where you want to be. "Destination" means:

- ❏ Your goals, dreams, objectives throughout life — what you want to achieve.

- ❏ The kind of place you want to be — the people you want to be with, the kind of person you want to become, the experiences you want to have, the quality of your life.

- ❏ Where you most care about arriving — the life that suits and expresses you.

Using the law of focus, that less is more, you need to think very carefully about the *particular, personal destination* that is best for you. To be happy, we each need a unique 80/20 destination, one that cuts out the great majority of trivial objectives and defines our own extremely relevant subset of vital objectives. Focusing on our 80/20 destination means solving the riddle of less is more for each individual. What are the few vital characteristics or results that will make us happiest? What are the very few qualities that we must focus on and multiply, not worrying about all the rest?

The 80/20 destination is a very small part of all available destinations, but the one that is central to our personality and deepest desires.

What happens when we truly focus on our 80/20 destination is that we make less more. If you are exceptionally selective and find the *few* things that *matter deeply* to you, life acquires a purpose and meaning way beyond what it had previously, when you were somewhat concerned about a large number of issues.

So who and what do you want to become? If you strip away all the acting and all the role-related trappings, who is the authentic you? What is your best 20 percent?

A good way to answer this question is to define your *20 percent spikes*. Let's take the example of my friend Steve, who runs a restaurant in Cape Town.

Steve's 20 percent skill and interest spikes (shown in Figure 5 on page 56) are entertainment, hospitality, rock music, starting businesses, teaching, understanding people, and verbal skills. He's ideally suited to starting and running a funky restaurant.

Figure 6 on page 57 depicts Steve's 20 percent emotional and personal spikes: inspiring leadership, teamwork, being trusted, and zest for life.

Use Figures 7 and 8 (pp. 58–9) to chart your own 20 percent spikes.

Put dots where you think they belong for each attribute and then join the lines up.

"I want to make a name for myself in the restaurant trade," Steve says, "not just in Cape Town and South Africa, but also internationally. I am committed to Tracy for life and to our children. I want them to grow up loved and to lead happy lives. Besides creating and building a new restaurant, I enjoy leading and training people so that they become the best they can be in their jobs. I'm still learning about what it takes to make a restaurant great and I will continue learning."

"Is there anything else," I ask, "that you really care about?"

"No," he says.

Steve knows his 80/20 destination.

Do you? Can you limit what you're trying to become and do, down to the essentials that really matter? If so, you can make less more.

Try filling in your destination below:

---

### My 80/20 destination is:

---

Check:

- ❏ Does the 80/20 destination reflect what you truly want and care about?

- ❏ Does it mirror your individuality? Is it unique to you?

- ❏ Does it bolster the best of your talents and emotions?

- ❏ Does it focus you? Will you avoid squandering energy on many other things? Does it exclude lots of objectives that currently soak up a large part of your energy?

- ❏ Is it short enough for you to remember all the time?

- ❏ Does it excite you? Is it a dream life for you?

But most importantly:

- ❏ Will pursuing it prove that less is more for you?

## Step 2: Find the 80/20 route

What's the best and easiest route to your 80/20 destination? Knowing what you want, how can you make a large improvement in your life while doing less overall?

- ❏ There are always many possible routes to any destination.

- ❏ A large majority of the routes will be greatly inferior to a few of the routes. The 80/20 routes we select are many times easier or more productive than other routes.

- ❏ There is always a route that provides an elegant and relatively easy solution, a way to get much more of what we want for

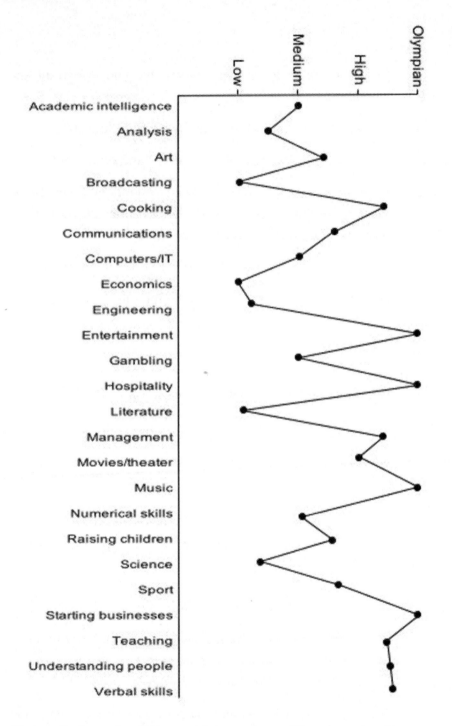

Figure 5  Steve's skills and interests — 20 percent spikes

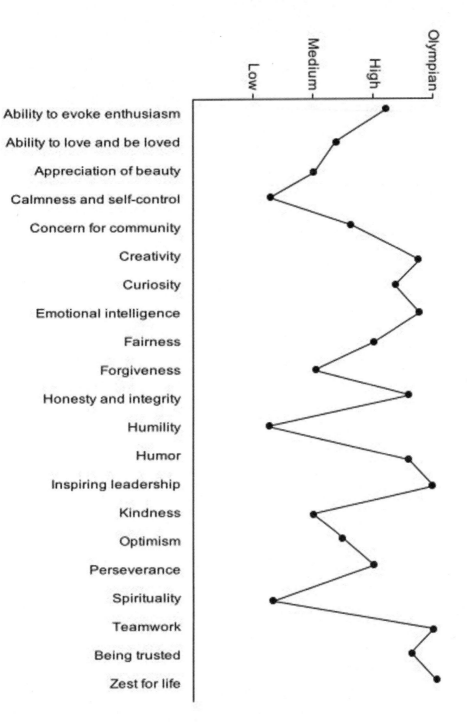

Figure 6  Steve's emotions and attributes — 20 percent spikes

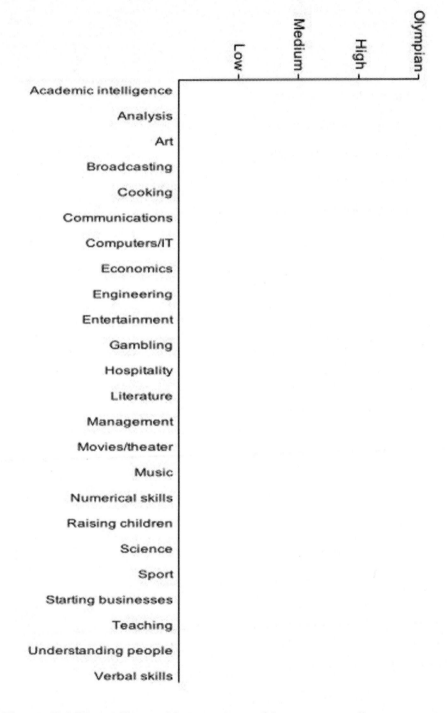

Figure 7  Your skills and interests — 20 percent spikes

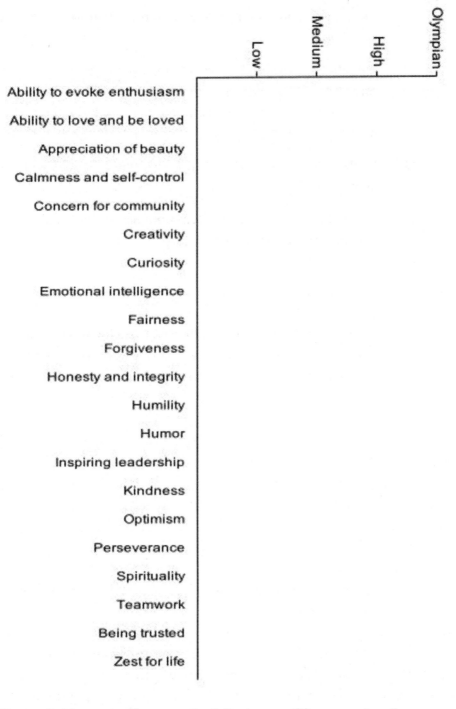

Figure 8  Your emotions and attributes — 20 percent spikes

much less energy, time, money, and bother. All we have to do is to find it.

❏ Probably, someone else has already discovered the route, or one very similar. Who has been spectacularly successful in reaching an objective similar to your 80/20 destination? How did they manage it?

❏ Routes are also personal affairs. Pick one that suits you particularly well.

❏ Routes become easier with help from allies. Think hitchhiking — who can give you a lift?

But the acid test of whether you've devised an 80/20 route is this:

❏ Does the route offer more with less? Does it give you not only a better solution, but also an easier one? Unless it is both better and easier, it won't lead to a major improvement in your life.

As a simple and literal illustration of routes, let's assume that your destination is Paddington train station in London. You live in East London, close to a tube (subway) stop. You like walking, but that is impractical: it's six miles and you need to get to Paddington quickly. Looking at the tube map, you plan to go directly from your local station on the Central Line to Notting Hill Gate, then change to the Circle Line for Paddington. All fine and dandy.

Yet what if you want a 80/20 route, which is both faster and also better? Try this. Leave the tube at Lancaster Gate station, two stops before Notting Hill Gate, and take a relaxed walk to Paddington, occupying no more than five minutes. Altogether you save yourself four stations traveling on the tube, as well as the hassle of changing from one line to another and waiting for a new train. The 80/20 route is easier, more pleasant, yet quicker too. More with less.

Or imagine you're in southern Spain, in a rush to get from San Pedro on the coast to Seville, three hours' drive inland. You're a nervous driver and usually get lost. The road to Seville starts with 30 miles of hairpin bends through a mountain pass to Ronda, then there are many changes of direction and the route is hard to follow. There is no other way to Seville that is anywhere near as short or direct. You grimly set off.

But what if you follow the 80/20 Way? You demand more with less: a solution that's easier for you, yet also takes less time. Even though it would take a few precious extra minutes, you study the map carefully, and ask the cashier at the service station for help. She tells you that for the price of a small toll, you can take the freeway to Malaga, then another freeway to Seville. How long will it take? Two hours, she says, if you drive fast. Is it clearly marked? Even your grandmother couldn't get lost, she laughs. You find she is right: the freeway is clearly marked and almost completely empty; the Spanish hate paying tolls.

By taking a little extra time to think, you've found a much easier route that is also faster. More with less.

Be clear, however, about your objectives before deciding the route. In the Seville example, the best route would be different if you had plenty of time, enjoyed driving on challenging roads, and placed a premium on beautiful scenery. If so, you'd pick the mountain route via Ronda: it would offer you more with less — more interest and stunning views for less distance and cost.

The "destination" is not only Seville, but also the fun of getting there. This is typical of life lived to the full. It's important to know what you want to achieve and what you *don't* want to achieve; and it is of equal or greater importance to know how you want to live, how you don't want to live, what person you want to be, and what person you don't want to be.

Of course, my travel examples are rather trivial. They are meant to provide simple and memorable illustrations of 80/20 routes and are not meant to imply that there's always a better travel plan or that one's touring routes are weighty enough to fret over. But for your key 80/20 destinations, it's worth substantial thought to devise a better and easier route, so that you get more with less. This is certainly the case for finding the route to your best 20 percent. How do we do this?

Back to Steve. Has he discovered his 80/20 route?

"I've made a start," he tells me. "I found a backer from overseas and I opened this restaurant two years ago. It won the best Cape Town restaurant competition last year and everyone agrees it is a cool place. But I want to have a chain of these restaurants in South Africa and then overseas. The first step is to open in Johannesburg. To do that I need to find a new backer and I'm close to having done that. Then I have to prove that the idea will work in Jo'burg."

"So is there nothing else important on the route?" I ask.

"There is one thing," Steve says. "I need a mentor from America or Europe or Australia. To get better at what I do, I need someone who's better than me to help stretch and stimulate me. I haven't found the mentor yet, but it's a key objective this year."

# What is the 80/20 route
# to your *best 20 percent?*

There are always many possible routes. The 80/20 route is the best, fastest, most fun, least worrisome, and least effortful way for you to get there. It is also — and here's the rub — the way you are *least* likely to be following now or to dream up on the spot.

Why? Because the 80/20 Way, like the 80/20 principle, is counterintuitive. It offers a *much better* answer simply because the right solution is not readily visible to us, conditioned as we are to take in the total picture, the "100 percent" of our experience. Left to our own devices, we'd devise a route that offers more for more. The challenge is to craft a route offering more for less.

Therefore, in finding the 80/20 route to your best 20 percent, try these eccentric questions:

❏ What's the route to your 80/20 destination that you would normally pursue? This is not the answer — instead, it's the standard against which you judge a possible 80/20 route. Unless you conjure up an approach that is hugely better than your habitual answer, you don't yet have your 80/20 route.

❏ Now ask, how can you make a vast improvement on your habitual answer, by unreasonably demanding more with less?

❏ Divide the improvement into two parts. First, how could you get more? What would be a much better way for you? What would you enjoy more, and what would get you to your 80/20 destination more quickly? Brainstorm all possible routes. If you're short of ideas, ask a friend or three to help — it's always easier to solve someone else's puzzle.

❏ Second, ask how the route could be made easier for you. Dream up many ideas.

❏ Then, put them together, until you have a way that might work and definitely offers more with less. Even if you're not sure it will work, try it. If it fails, move on to your second choice of route — but only if it too offers more with less.

If you're stumped for an answer, go back to your 20 percent spikes. The things that you are best at, that come naturally to you, will give clues on how you can best get more with less.

For example, earlier in my life, my 80/20 destination was to become a successful and well-paid management consultant. The first route I tried seemed very promising: I landed a job with one of the best and fastest-growing American firms, the Boston Consulting Group (BCG). Sadly (or, as it later turned out, happily), though my clients seemed to like me, my bosses didn't. I just about managed to resign before I got fired.

The second route I devised was to join Bain & Company, a spinoff from BCG. Having failed the first time round, with a huge dent to my ego, I determined to correct the things that had sunk me before: my lazy style, independence of spirit, irreverence, and reputation for frivolity. I decided to make a big deal of working unbelievably hard, brownnosing my bosses, and presenting the serious and responsible side of my nature. I would not fail again and I would prove the folks at BCG wrong in their judgment of me.

Was this the right thing to do? Yes and no. Bain was a fine choice. It had a great business formula, exclusively focused on serving the top person in any client organization, and grew even faster than BCG. Talent was so thin on the ground in Bain that I rapidly got promoted to junior partner. I reined in my rebel instincts, projecting a convincing image of company loyalist and team builder.

I was heading nicely along to my 80/20 destination, but one day I stopped to think, what was I doing? Was I really following an 80/20 route?

Clearly not. In donning my Bain mask, I was seeking more with more. More success, more interesting work, more responsibility, more money. Fine. But the bargain I struck had me putting in more too: more intense work, more hours, more single-minded devotion to the job and firm, more politicking, more worry, more conformity to the bosses' predilections, and more wearisome international travel. For someone who believed in more with less, this was far from ideal.

What about my 20 percent spikes? Was I playing properly to these? Alas, no. I'm good at ideas, sudden insight, spotting talent, and telling clients what to do to make more money. I'm bad at sustained hard work (I'm a sprinter, not a long-distance runner), appearing grave and serious, internal politics, and the whole messy business of managing other people. Was Bain the right place for me? Not really. I was not straitlaced or loyal enough. Was I finding it a strain to appear so Bain-like? You bet.

My first thought was that I had enough money and should take life easier, get out of management consulting altogether. That would be less with less: less work, less strain and stress, but also less money and less interesting work. I hadn't yet reached my 80/20 destination and I still wanted to prove that I could get there. Besides, I professed to believe in more with less.

So how was I going to contrive more with less? What did I want? I wanted less angst, less conformity, less suppression of my true nature, less travel, less intense work, fewer administrative duties, and fewer bosses (preferably none at all!). I wanted more work with interesting clients, more independence, more time with my family and friends, more freedom to select my colleagues, and also — let's be honest — even more money.

To state my desires was to answer them. In spelling out what more and less I wanted, the 80/20 route rapidly became clear. The only way I could get more with less, the exact way I wanted it, was to start my own firm. And yet, this wasn't quite true. On thinking deeper, I realized that I didn't want the administrative responsibility of having Koch & Co, nor did I think I had the full set of skills to found a truly preeminent firm. The ideal 80/20 route for me was to co-found a firm, with two other partners *whose 20 percent spikes exactly complemented mine.*

I firmly believe that the most ambitious destination and route can also be the easiest — if and only if they precisely match your strengths. In working at Bain & Co, I successfully corrected my weaknesses, but really only papered over the most evident cracks. Correcting our weaknesses, the most we become is mediocre. If we hone our few super-strengths, our 20 percent spikes, insist on behavior that is authentic and true to our inner selves, and unreasonably demand more with less, the sky is the limit.

## Step 3: Take 80/20 action

What is 80/20 action and how does it differ from the actions we normally take in life? There are three liberating differences:

- ❏ 80/20 action is dictated by your unique 80/20 destination and 80/20 route.

- ❏ 80/20 action focuses on the very few actions that are proven to give you the great majority of your happiness and fulfillment: less is more.

- ❏ 80/20 action involves less total action and greater total results — more with less.

Once I had decided my 80/20 destination (to be a successful management consultant) and my 80/20 route (to start a new firm with two partners), the 80/20 action was obvious. There were only two actions necessary: to find the partners, and then start the firm! Once I had made my decision, all the other actions I was taking every day became the *trivial many*; finding the partners and starting the firm became the *vital few*. Though it wasn't clear how I was going to take those two actions, they were all I really thought and cared about.

Here's the eerie thing: Two months after I made my decision, I'd still not taken the 80/20 action. I couldn't decide which of my colleagues to approach about starting a competing firm — a wrong move could find me out of a job. Then chance intervened. I called Ian Fisher, a colleague and friend, about our current project, and at the end of the call he let something slip.

"There's something weird going on with Jim and Iain [two other junior partners]. We can't really speak about it, but they made a sudden trip to Boston [Bain & Co's headquarters]."

"What's going on, Ian?"

"I can't tell you, Richard, but it's really strange and it's really bad."

"What do you mean you can't tell me, we're close colleagues, and come to that, I'm your boss."

"Bill Bain made me swear not to tell anyone."

[Me, taking a wild guess] "Have they resigned?"

Silence. After a long pause, "You said that. I didn't."

Jim Lawrence's phone rang and rang. Iain Evans' phone was off the hook. I jumped on my bicycle and rode along the Thames towpath to his home in Kew. I found them holed up together, shell-shocked after a traumatic encounter with Bill Bain. Were they going to start a new firm? Yes. Could I be their partner? Maybe. Yes.

Chance had taken my 80/20 action for me. Or had it?

There's a marvelous sentence in Paulo Coelho's fable *The Alchemist*:

When you want something,

*all the universe conspires*

in helping you to

*achieve* it.

I think that is right: when you are clear about your 80/20 destination and 80/20 route, then chance events will give your plans a mighty shove in the right direction. But the key phrase is *when you know your destiny*.

If I hadn't known my 80/20 destination and 80/20 route, I wouldn't have pressed Ian Fisher about his cryptic remarks, I probably wouldn't have guessed what had happened, and I wouldn't have — apparently impulsively — jumped on my bike (it was a long ride and I had other plans that morning). I still had to take action, but actions are easier if you've narrowed the field down to an obsession that is right for you.

Action doesn't always have to be preplanned. Desire *does* have to be preplanned. Being open to chance events, and interpreting and exploiting them properly, is part of the 80/20 Way.

Ultimately, if you don't take the few 80/20 actions, your life won't be transformed. If you do take them, they can multiply happiness out of all proportion to the effort.

Make the most of your difference. Nobody else can. Focus on the best of yourself, so that less is more. Find the route to transform your life, so you get more results with less worry and less effort. Then act, and be open to the great luck that the universe will try to bestow on you. When you've discovered and selected the authentic parts of yourself and made them work smoothly and easily, you'll be unique, highly valuable... and yes, very happy too.

# *Enjoy Work and Success*

It's true hard work never killed anyone, but I figure, why take the chance?

Ronald Reagan

Remember the Woody Allen movie *The Purple Rose of Cairo*? Mia Farrow is sitting in the audience, watching her favorite film. Suddenly actor Jeff Daniels, bored with reciting the same lines time and again, jumps from the movie into the cinema. He snatches Mia Farrow off, unleashing a fabulous love affair.

There, I think, lies the secret of success. I don't mean grabbing Mia Farrow, I mean the ability to switch between ordinary life and life as it could be. I mean having an idea, or a fantasy, or a passion — and acting on it. Stepping out of a life of duty, where everything runs on predictable lines dictated by other people, into a life created by your own imagination. Forgetting about hard work and using the greatest of all human attributes, our ability to move between the world as it is and the world in our minds. Thinking, imagining, creating, enjoying.

Other animals can work hard, only humans can *think* hard. Other animals are programmed by evolution. People are too, but we can also program ourselves and change the world we find into a world we prefer. The whole edifice of modern civilization rests not on drudgery, muscle power, repetition, or long hours of work, but on insight, inspiration, inventiveness, originality, and enterprise. On moving between where we are now, in the real world, and the world we dream up in our minds and then make real.

What is true for humanity as a whole is also true for individuals. The most successful people change the world not through sweat and tears but through ideas and passion. It is not a matter of hard work or time on the job; it is having a different view, an original idea, something that expresses their individuality and creativity. Success comes from thinking, then acting on those thoughts.

So if you believe you have to work hard and do unpleasant things to be successful, think again. Do you imagine that Bill Gates, former college dropout and founder of Microsoft, became the world's richest man through hard graft? Do you think that Warren Buffett, the master investor and world's second-richest person, works very hard? What about media moguls Oprah Winfrey and Rupert Murdoch? What's different about them? Devotion to hard slog or great new ideas?

What about Ronald Reagan? John F Kennedy? Winston Churchill? Albert Einstein? Charles Darwin? William Shakespeare? Christopher Columbus? Jesus Christ?

These giants weren't chained to their desks. What they all did was to spend time on what mattered to them, on a few essentials where they exerted leadership, and little or no time on the mass of trivia occupying their hard-working contemporaries.

There is the difficult way to success and there is the easier way.

The difficult way is to study hard and for a long time, work hard for 60 hours or more a week for several decades, worry about the impression you're giving, and claw your way up some organizational pyramid. Sacrifice a pleasant life now in the hope of a much more pleasant future life. Try to do extraordinary things, at extraordinary cost, to get extraordinary results.

The 80/20 Way is easier. It's open to everyone, including those who are far behind in the education and career stakes.

Make a great mental leap: dissociate effort from reward. Focus on the outcomes that you want and find the easiest way to them with *least effort*, *least sacrifice,* and *most pleasure.* Concentrate on what produces extraordinary results *without* extraordinary effort. Be efficient but relaxed. First, think results. Then get them with least energy:

❏ 20 percent of work, effort, and resources give over 80 percent of results. What gives us the 80 percent outcome for 20 percent effort — or the 400 percent outcome for 100 percent effort? What's the *ordinary* way to *extraordinary* results?

❏ Over 80 percent of people struggle to achieve 20 percent of results. Fewer than 20 percent of people commandeer 80 percent of the goodies. In your area, who are they? What do they do differently?

❏ 80 percent of your value to other people comes from 20 percent or less of what you do. What are these few vital activities?

❏ 80 percent of your success derives from 20 percent or less of your skills and knowledge. What are the really valuable things that you do so much better than other people?

❏ 80 percent of your achievements arrive in 20 percent or fewer of the *circumstances* in which you find yourself. You shine at specific times, in particular ways, with certain people. When? Where? Why?

❏ 80 percent of what you want comes from 20 percent of the *tactics or behavior* that you adopt. What behavior has results out of all proportion to energy?

❏ For anything you attempt, one *way of doing it* is markedly superior: a route delivering 80 percent of results for 20 percent of normal effort. Experiment until you've found a way that is four times better than before.

## *Intelligent and lazy*

German military chief General von Manstein said:

> "There are only four types of officers.
>
> First, there are the lazy, stupid ones. Leave them alone, they do no harm.
>
> Second, there are the hard-working intelligent ones. They make excellent staff officers, ensuring that every detail is properly considered.
>
> Third, there are the hard-working, stupid ones. These people are a menace, and must be fired at once. They create irrelevant work for everybody.
>
> Finally, there are the intelligent lazy ones. They are suited for the highest office."

Cultivate lazy intelligence. Do you lack smarts or lack laziness?

If you think you're not so smart — and to think this, you have to be quite intelligent after all — work on your knowledge and expertise in a very narrow area, where extraordinary results are available for modest effort.

If you are smart, but not lazy, work on laziness. To do everything, simply because you can, lowers effectiveness. Concentrate on the really important things that get amazing results. Do only the few things with greatest benefit.

It's amazing how often people dispute this advice. A typical conversation runs like this:

> Friend: "You must be joking when you say become lazier."
>
> Me: "I'm deadly serious. I can't focus well enough on the 20 percent if I'm also trying to do everything else. Far better to spend twice as much time on the magic 20 percent, and far less on the rest. Bottom line: 60 percent more results for 60 percent less energy."

Friend: "Shouldn't we put 100 percent energy into the magic 20 percent and get four times more?"

Me: "Fine in theory, and in practice eventually, but first slow down. Stop inessential things. There's a limit to how much time we can spend on the magic activities without diluting quality. *Force* ourselves to do less. Win time to find more vital areas to work on and more effective things to do."

Friend: "But you don't really believe in being lazy, do you?"

Me: "There are lazy people, like Ronald Reagan, who achieved a great deal just by being focused on one or two objectives. And there are super-hard workers, like President Carter, who had too many objectives and failed frenetically. Still, there are excellent scientists or artists, obsessed with their work, who love it. I wouldn't tell them to become lazy. I'm not really advocating laziness, but time to concentrate on what matters. If you don't like the word 'lazy,' try 'relaxed.' Do what you enjoy, do it calmly and without worries.

"A hard-working person is often too busy to spot what's really significant. A lazy person wants to do as little as possible and so concentrates only on the essentials. What's really productive is a lazy person who thinks new thoughts and is focused on making them happen. Thinking is often disturbing, sometimes even frightening. Burying ourselves in trivia is less threatening.

"For most of us, the only way to create something new and valuable is to slow down, do fewer things, chill out. If you really love what you're doing, you don't need to be lazy. If you're doing lots of things you don't enjoy, cut them, keeping just the valuable and enjoyable things."

# What do super-successful people do differently?

If we want to be successful, we should see what is different about the "stars." I can see six common characteristics:

## *The stars are ambitious*

No surprise here. Yet their ambition is sweet and unforced. Because...

## *The stars love what they do*

Ronald Reagan had the time of his life as Governor of California and over eight White House years. Top authors adore writing in exotic locations. High flyers are vibrant, full of life, overflowing with quiet pleasure or infectious exuberance.

Researcher Srully Blotnick investigated self-made millionaires. He discovered that they loved their work. Their passion took them to the top.

Enjoyment, not effort or education, is the key to success. Hurrah!

Picture millions slaving on the educational treadmill. Or working in dark Satanic towers for pinch-mouthed bosses and mean-spirited corporations. Could they all be barking up the wrong tree?

If that's you, rejoice! Throw off your chains. Find something you love doing.

And if that's not you, rejoice too! The treadmill ain't necessary. Most successful entrepreneurs had no university education, usually no further education at all. More than half left school as soon as they could. It was enthusiasm that made them.

It can make you too. Those winners' school grades were poor, but didn't bar them from success. They found something they loved doing, where they could create something that other people wanted. You can do the same. Is there something you love doing that could become your business or profession?

## *The stars are lopsided*

Stars are not all-rounders. The top people have massive strengths — and equally massive downsides. Their weaknesses don't matter. What leads to extraordinary results is concentration on the strengths, honing these to Olympian standards.

*Where* you work — the profession, firm, department, job — is crucial.

If 20 percent of potential jobs and professions yield 80 percent of the potential benefit, seek jobs where your lopsided strength comes to the fore. Balance is mediocrity.

## *The stars know a lot about a little*

Have you been told to gain broad experience? Don't. Focus all your energy on one area.

Become expert on a narrow front. Know 99 percent about 1 percent of something. Meet all the experts. See how they work, what kind of lives they lead. Mimic them.

## *The stars think and communicate clearly*

They sell and market themselves concisely.

How can you learn this? Do a stint as a salesperson.

Selling is tough. It invites rejection. It also teaches you how to accept rejection, get on with different folks, communicate, and negotiate effectively.

Sell anything — autos, hi-fis, computers, advertising space, magazine subscriptions, anything at all — for a few months. You'll learn to sell yourself, an essential life skill. The rest of your life will be so much easier and more successful!

## The stars evolve their own success formula

Does your favorite comedian have a unique formula? Is it timing, tone of voice, material used, or something else distinctive? Whatever, it's imitable and invaluable.

The stars didn't arrive at their formula overnight. Neither need you. Observe many formulae. Adapt or combine them or invent your own. Experiment. See what delivers *more with less*.

# The 80/20 Way to enjoy work and success

## Step 1: Focus on your 80/20 destination

*What do you really want from your work?* What does it mean to you? What would be ideal? What are the few things you care most about?

Below are many different things that might be important about your job.

### WHAT REALLY MATTERS TO ME ABOUT MY WORK?

- ❏     High pay

- ❏     A job I enjoy

- ❏     Security

- ❏     Good, comfortable conditions

- ❏     Excitement

- ❏     Friends at work, interesting colleagues

- ❏     Makes me think

- ❏     Variety

- ❏     A decent boss

❏ Hours that fit in with my life and are not too long

❏ Freedom to do things my own way

❏ Employer's reputation

❏ Prestige of my own job

❏ Excellent fringe benefits

❏ Prospects for promotion

❏ Important work that benefits other people

❏ Good training and ability to add to my skills

❏ An inspiring boss or leader in the organization

❏ Flexible hours, work when I like

❏ Place where I might meet my life's love

❏ Work that exactly fits my own abilities

❏

❏

❏

The bottom three bullets are left blank for you to fill in anything else you want.

Tick all the bullets that matter to you.

Now, remembering the need to focus and that less is more, pick the one, two, or three points — ideally just one point — that matter(s) most to your happiness. Your choice points toward your 80/20 destination for work. If you can be even more specific — "I want to be a movie director," "I want to be a nurse," "I want to be a management consultant" — so much the better.

**W**hat is really strange is that many talented people pursue jobs and careers that do *not* make them and their families happy — or as happy as a different job and career could.

Of my good friends, I figure at least half have not chosen the career path that would make them happiest. They put success and money ahead of enjoyment, fulfillment, and purpose.

Most of them have made good money. Did the extra happiness from money and status outweigh the extra happiness they would have derived from more fulfilling work? I doubt it.

Here's an intriguing fact. Dividing my friends into those who chose the jobs they loved on the one hand, and those who worked for money and success on the other, it is the former group who have made, on average, more money. Those who worked for fun and fulfillment rather than money also tended to make more money.

# Work is more fun

## than *fun.*

Noel Coward said that. Now hard evidence backs him up.

Psychologist Mihaly Csikszentmihalyi has pioneered research into "flow," those moments of peak happiness when time stands still, when you find yourself doing exactly what you want to be doing, never wanting it to end, rather like the happiness islands discussed earlier.

He says that Americans derive much more flow from work than from leisure time. Flow derives from a sense of personal mastery and active achievement. Work that is matched to our strengths — that leads to clear and positive results — gives enormous satisfaction.

Success is not, and should not be seen as, a desperate process of piling up wealth and conspicuous consumption of material goods in order to impress other people. This is a game which nobody — except perhaps Bill

Gates for a limited time — can win. A millionaire's conspicuous consumption is dwarfed by a billionaire's, setting off a never-ending chain of competition and envy that destroys our benevolence, drains our energy, and is far removed from anyone's authentic needs and desires.

In success as in everything else, less is more. Quality is more valuable than quantity, giving is more satisfying than consuming, abundant time trumps abundant goods, serenity is better than striving, and love given generates love received. What we all want deep down is abundant time, security, affection, peace, tranquility, spiritual awareness, self-confidence, and a sense that we are expressing ourselves and creating things of great value to other people. True success is being able to spend our time how we like, fulfilling our unique talent, being valuable to people we value, and being loved.

Be very clear, therefore, what success means for you and seek that, not the world's definition of success, a tawdry, second-hand concept that everyone professes to believe but nobody actually experiences and enjoys.

You don't always have to change your job to enjoy it more. Maybe you can simply change the way you do it.

My barber and my tennis coach tell me about their lives and ask me about mine; I get free therapy with every haircut and tennis lesson! They enjoy their work more this way.

My mother, who used to be a nurse, was just in hospital for a week. She remarked how much more nurses today chat to the patients and their families, involving them in restoring the patient to health.

Could you do something to add meaning and value to your job?

IS THE IDEA WE CAN ENJOY WORK JUST PIE IN THE SKY?
Not everyone agrees that they can enjoy their work. My friend
Bruce complains about his work. He took me to task when I said,
"Get a job you like."

"As far as I'm concerned," he said, "what you say is pie in
the sky. I don't like my job, but at least it's permanent and
secure, which is a lot these days. I don't think you understand
how tough it is in today's workplace, especially for those of us
without qualifications. Haven't you heard about casualization? All
the permanent jobs are being replaced by contracts and casual
positions. I'm just hoping to hang on to my job — that's the peak
of my ambition. The idea of having a career I love is just a pipe
dream."

"Let's look at it this way," I countered. "A hundred years
ago, work was grim and tedious. Nobody stopped to ask whether
they could enjoy it. But today millions of people revel in their
work. And the more they love it, the more successful they are.
Why don't you do the same?

"Finding a job you enjoy may be hard and take a long time,"
I added, "but it is always possible. Every single person I know who
has really tried to find a job they love has managed it eventually.
Almost nothing you do, Bruce, will affect your happiness for your
whole life more than finding a job you like. It's worth using all
your effort and imagination on this."

"How can you say that you can always get a nice job," Bruce
said, "when unemployment's shooting up and good jobs are like gold
dust?"

"Well," I said, "that's true, but even with high unemployment, there are always jobs. There is always hope. Why not make
a list of jobs that you know or suspect you'd enjoy? Spend a lot of
time on this: make a really long list. Think whether you could create your own job.

"I have lots of acquaintances who've been through this sequence. First they're fired or retire from a job they dislike. Eventually they create their own job, one they like, either by persuading someone else to employ them, or through self-employment. Out of desperation, really, as they'd zero chance of a normal job.

"Either they make a go of that job or it doesn't work out, but they make it at their second or third try. They nearly always end up relishing their new work. Often make a small fortune too. Isn't it better to go through this process without being fired and when you're still quite young?"

"Maybe," Bruce said, "but the jobs I'd like have hundreds of better-qualified people going for them."

"It's true," I said, "you'll compete against many people for a great job, but motivation matters hugely. Whether you really want the job or not shows through more than people imagine. There can be 20 percent unemployment in a category and yet if someone is 100 percent more motivated, they'll get that job or a similar one sooner or later.

"Many friends have jobs they don't like because they're secure, or they pay well, or they get pressure from their wife, husband, partner, parents, peers, or teachers. Other friends have moved to jobs they like that pay less well, and found some way of dealing with the money — by downscaling their spending, having two or more workers in the family, or using savings. What generally happens is that they and their families are happier right away. *None* of them regretted it. After a time, many made more money too."

## *Step 2: Find your 80/20 route*

Look for more with less: super-returns on your energy. In every organization, in every industry, in every profession, some people are getting ahead much faster than others, without working harder. Why? Look for the 20 percent that delivers 80 percent:

❏ Fewer than 20 percent of applicants for any job are seriously considered and they get 100 percent of the jobs. What will put you in the magic 20 percent? Do you need experience from another job *before* applying for the job you really want?

❏ 80 percent of fun is concentrated in 20 percent of jobs. If you want fun, go for one of these.

❏ 80 percent of jobs that are fun and pay well are concentrated in very few professions and organizations. It may take some working out, but which jobs that appeal to you also pay extremely well? Do you passionately want to land one of those great jobs? Prepare a long campaign.

❏ 80 percent of growth comes from 20 percent of organizations. To get ahead, work for the fastest-growing firm. *Someone* has to fill all those new opportunities.

❏ 80 percent of promotions come in 20 percent of fast-growth firms or firms that always promote from within. Many family-run firms do that.

❏ 80 percent of promotions come from 20 percent of bosses — those who are going places themselves. Who you work for may matter more than what you do. Put yourself in a rising star's slipstream. When was the last time your boss was promoted? If you can't remember, find another boss.

❏  80 percent of results come from 20 percent of activities. What are the things that truly produce results in your work? Do more of them. Do them better. Forget everything else.

❏  80 percent of useful experience in an industry or profession comes from working with 20 percent or fewer practitioners and from working in 20 percent or fewer organizations. Are you where you'll learn most and fastest with least effort? Do you have the right bosses and mentors?

❏  20 percent or perhaps much less of what *you* do creates 80 percent or more of your value. Are you in the right place: right role, right industry, right organization, right unit? Where could you create the most value? What's the ideal job for *you*? Does it exist already? How can you work toward creating it?

❏  80 percent of promotions come from impressing a few people. Who are they for the job you want? How can you best impress them?

❏  80 percent of profits come from fewer than 20 percent of customers. Who are they for you? Could you serve these customers exclusively?

❏  80 percent of wealth and wellbeing is created by fewer than 20 percent of people. Who are they in your area? How do you become one? Could you get together and spin off a profit center or new firm?

❏  Could you "employ" the best and brightest people, as boss or owner?

❏  80 percent of value is created by concentrating on 20 percent of *issues* within a market, by *innovating* accordingly. 80 percent of value comes from 20 percent of changes. What demands are changing? Who is driving progress? How? Could you copy it, do it cheaper, take it to a new place, or take it further?

Which route will take you to your 80/20 destination for work and success:

❑ faster than you would normally reckon?

❑ to a much higher level than you're aiming at now?

❑ without cutting across your personality, forcing you to do things that are inauthentic or that you don't like, or making you play an artificial role?

❑ using your most distinctive and exceptional 20 percent spikes?

❑ enjoyably?

By definition, an 80/20 route must fulfill *all* these conditions and fully excite you. Keep thinking until you've found *your* 80/20 route to enjoy work and success.

## Step 3: Take 80/20 action

Work out the three key 80/20 *actions* to get you started. Each one must take you a substantial or giant leap along your 80/20 route toward your 80/20 destination.

Write them opposite.

For every 80/20 action step, stop three or four other actions. Act less; focus more.

Is this hard? Change is strange. Yet you're trading many things you don't care about for the few things you love. This change is progress.

The secret of trying any new approach is to take one action and find that it works. This will encourage you to take another step that works, and then another...

80/20 Action 1:

80/20 Action 2:

80/20 Action 3:

In the First World War, sailors whose ships had sunk floated around in lifeboats, cold and hungry, for days, sometimes for a week or so. Then they'd start to die. The mystery was that a greater proportion of the *younger* sailors died first.

How could this be? The young mariners were fitter and should have lasted longer. Eventually it was realized that many older men had been sunk before, or knew a colleague who'd been sunk and had been rescued alive. Simply knowing that they'd been saved before reinforced the will to live. They knew there was a route to survival. They didn't fret or worry. They knew that hanging on to life worked.

It was decided to brief all crew that they might be stuck in lifeboats for many days, yet that they would then likely be rescued alive. Survival rates soared.

Like the sailors anticipating rescue, if you put just one or two well-thought-through 80/20 actions into practice, you'll find that they work. So act now, and gain confidence that less is more and more with less really can change your life.


## A HERO FROM ZERO

I'd like to close this chapter with a story about someone whose entire life turned on less is more and more with less.

A long time ago a chap called Rowland taught in his father's school. He then became a clerk in the South Australian Commission. There was nothing remarkable about Rowland. He wasn't well off, well known, or well connected.

But he had an idea.

In his day, it was extremely expensive to receive a letter. The further the distance, the more it cost the recipient. Rowland's weird idea was that if the price of sending a letter could be slashed to a very low level, then thousands more people would send letters. He also invented the idea of a "stamp" — the person sending the letter would pay, allowing delivery without the mailman having to collect money.

Rowland Hill persuaded the British government to experiment. In 1840 the penny post — featuring the "penny black" stamp — was born. It was a huge success. Hill became head of the new postal service, rich, and famous.

Fifty countries followed suit within a decade. This new communication channel was as revolutionary as the internet nowadays. The penny post encouraged ordinary people to learn to read and write, turbo-charging popular education.

Though he didn't know it, Rowland followed the 80/20 Way. More postal revenues came from slashing the price. One simple idea and one 80/20 action led to huge social benefit and a great new career.

Ask yourself:

Could I dream up an idea like Rowland Hill? One that will benefit lots of people and perhaps change my life too?

# Unmask the Mystery of Money

The greatest force in the world? Compound interest.

Albert Einstein

A famous financial adviser spoke to a money management class about a great book, *The Richest Man in Babylon* by Paul Glason.

"There is really only one message in this book," the financial guru said, "and it's still true today — to have no future financial worries, all you need to do is to save and invest 10 percent of your income for long-term growth."

The lecturer asked the group — who had paid good money to learn how to straighten out their finances — who'd read the book. About two-thirds of the audience put up their hands.

"Please keep your hands up for the moment," he said. "Now, everyone who's followed the key message of the book — saved and invested 10 percent of their income — please leave their hands up, and the rest put your hands down."

Out of about 100 people with their hands up, every single one put them down. They'd all understood and agreed with the message. It mattered to them. Yet *none of them had taken the simple action necessary.*

How come? To some extent, because action is always more difficult than thinking about action. But to a larger extent, because Paul Glason's book didn't provide an easy method for saving.

I'll make a deal with you. I'll provide an easy way out of money problems, provided that you promise to take it — to act on the easy answer. If you're not prepared to take my proposed deal, skip this chapter, because you won't derive any benefit from reading it.

Three mysteries of money have baffled people from time immemorial:

❏ Why do a few people have most money and most people have very little?

❏ Is there a reliable way to make all the money you need?

❏ Can money buy happiness? If not, what's the point of it?

The good news is that money's mystery can be unmasked.

## VILFREDO'S EARTH-SHATTERING DISCOVERY

Over 100 years ago, a shaggy-haired Italian economist got a real shock. Professor Vilfredo Pareto of Lausanne University was investigating wealth in Britain. He found a curiously lopsided picture: a few people had most of the money.

Then he looked at statistics on British wealth in earlier centuries. Every time, he got an almost identical picture.

Pareto compared wealth in America, in Italy, in France, in Switzerland, and elsewhere. For every country with statistics, the same result. A law of money operated everywhere, any time.

Pareto explained his law badly. Not until 1950 did Joseph Juran rename it the 80/20 principle: 20 percent of people enjoyed 80 percent of money.

In Pareto's time, taxes were very low. In the last century, governments around the world taxed the rich to give to the poor.

Yet Pareto's picture hasn't budged. The wealthiest 20 percent of Americans own 84 percent of money. The planet's top 20 percent corner 85 percent of money. These numbers are shocking. Money — and the 80/20 principle — are more powerful than governments.

## Why do 20 percent own 84 percent?

Money is a force, like the wind, the waves, and the weather. Money dislikes being equally distributed. Money clones money.

Why? How can we attract money?

Money obeys the 80/20 principle because of compound interest — Einstein's "most powerful force in the universe."

Start with a small dollop of money, save and invest it, then compound interest will do the rest.

In 1946 Anne Scheiber, who knew little about money, put $5,000 into the stock market. She locked away the share certificates and stopped worrying. By 1995 her modest nest egg had transmogrified into $22,000,000 — up 440,000 percent! All courtesy of compound interest.

If we never save money, we will always be poor, *no matter how much money we earn.*

Most people have very little money because they don't save. The typical 50-year-old American has earned a great deal but has savings of just $2,300.

People with the most money have typically saved and invested it for many years. Compound interest multiplies savings in a breathtaking way.

## HOW ANYONE CAN MAKE A MILLION

"Is it really true," asks Aaron, my personal assistant, "that I could become rich?"

"Yes," I say, "if you do one simple thing."

"Come off it, Richard, that can't be true." Enter Alison, Aaron's younger friend. Alison is a hairdresser with pink, punkish hair. "If it was easy, we'd all be millionaires. You know as well as me that there are a few people with all this," she waves at the swimming pool, lush gardens, and tennis court, "and then there are all the rest of us, struggling with money."

Aaron, Alison, and I are basking in November sunshine, sipping ice-cold drinks at my house in Spain. I make the most of my captive audience.

"You're right," I tell Alison, "most people — even with big jobs and incomes to match — don't have much spare cash. I don't say it's easy to accumulate money. I just say it's possible for everyone."

"So what's the secret?"

"Aaron is 23, right? Assume he saves $200 a month..."

"Pigs will fly," said Alison.

"Maybe," I say, "but imagine he saves and invests $200 a month, and it grows at 10 percent a year for 42 years, until he's 65. How much would Aaron have then? $200 a month is $2,400 a year — times 42 is $100,000 and change. But you have to add the growth on top.

"So," I face Aaron, "what's your guess?"

"Maybe double that. $200,000? Alison?"

"I'm no good at sums," she says, "but it couldn't be that much. Maybe $150,000?"

"The right answer," I reveal, "is over $1.4 million." They're stunned.

"But that assumes Aaron could save 10 percent — I don't believe that..."

"Fine, I'll come to that later," I interrupt, "but Alison, what about you?"

"Harrumph," she says. "Nobody earns less than me. You know how little hairdressers get? Worst-paid profession. Wouldn't be worth saving."

"How old are you? How much do you earn?"

"Eighteen. $16,000 a year. A tenth is $1,600. If I saved that, which I don't think I could, what would my nest egg become?"

I produce calculator and paper. The computer is faster, but I want to demonstrate the sums. Aaron fetches more drinks. When he's back, I'm ready.

"Whaddyathink? If Alison saved $1,600 a year till 65, what would she have?"

Aaron grabs the calculator. $1,600 times 47 years equals around $75,000. He multiplies that by five, his estimate for compound interest. "$400,000," he guesses.

"No way," Alison shrieks. "Can't be more than $250,000."

"Have I got news for you," I tell her. Clichés seem to be expected. "The right answer is $1.5 million."

"Impossible," she snorts. "I earn much less than Aaron, there's not much difference in our age, you say I'd get more than him. Calculator must be glitched."

"No," I say. "It makes sense. The compounding is so powerful, just a few extra years make all the difference. It's more important to start saving early than to earn a lot."

"It's all just numbers until you say how we save 10 percent of our pay," said Alison. "Don't see how we can, we always spend more than we earn."

"I'll come to that later," I said. And I will. But first, should we care about money?

# Can money buy *happiness?*

## Yes, if you're *poor.*

"Money is better than poverty," Woody Allen quipped, "if only for financial reasons." If we're starving or homeless, money can bring a better life.

But beyond a certain point — a surprisingly low point — more money doesn't deliver more happiness.

A study of tens of thousands of people in 29 countries compared average life satisfaction in each country with average purchasing power (see Figure 9).[1] It showed that in poor countries, purchasing power and life satisfaction are clearly related. Yet once countries are half as rich as America, there is absolutely no relationship between money and happiness.

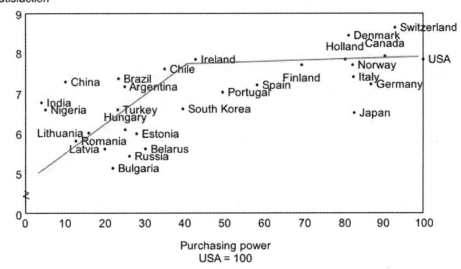

Figure 9  Life satisfaction and purchasing power in 29 countries

Looking within individual countries bears this out. Very poor Americans are less happy, but otherwise money does not affect happiness. Being one of the 100 richest Americans adds only a smidgeon to happiness.

Or consider a study of 22 lottery jackpot winners, who showed initial euphoria. It didn't last. Within a year, the winners were no happier than before.

More evidence: real purchasing power in three rich countries doubled between 1950 and 2000, yet happiness levels didn't rise at all. As countries become wealthier, depression soars, with victims also suffering at a much younger age.

The evidence is overwhelming. Being moderately well off means that you are happier than if you were very poor. But once you are well fed, clothed, and housed, getting wealthier probably won't make you happier.

In the nineteenth century, John Stuart Mill gave one excellent reason for this being true — *we don't want to be rich, we just want to be richer than other people.* When our living standard improves but everyone else's does too, we don't feel better off. We forget that our cars and houses are better than before, because our friends all drive similar cars and have just as pleasant homes.

Right now, I'm living in South Africa. Here, I feel rich. In Europe or America, I don't. My feeling has nothing to do with how well off I am and everything to do with how well off other people are. Living standards are much lower in South Africa, so I feel wealthy.

There's also the pain and hassle of making money. On April 8, 1991, *Time* magazine's cover story highlighted the price paid for successful careers:

❏ 61 percent of 500 professionals said that "earning a living today requires so much effort that it's difficult to find time to enjoy life."

❏ 38 percent said that they were cutting back on sleep to earn more money.

❏ 69 percent said they'd like to "slow down and live a more relaxed life"; only 19 percent wanted "a more exciting, faster-paced life."

❏ 56 percent wanted to find more time for personal interests and hobbies, and 89 percent said it was important to them to spend more time with their families, something that their careers made difficult.

How are we doing now? Have many of us fled the rat race? Nah. We're still chasing more money for more time. The average working American now works 2,000 hours a year. That's two weeks more than in 1980! And the average middle-income couple with children now work 3,918 hours between them — seven weeks more than just 10 years ago.

More money can be a trap, leading to more spending, more commitments, more worry, more complexity, more time on administering money, more desires, more time at work, less choice about how we spend our time, and degradation of our independence and life energy. Our lifestyle locks us into our "workstyle."

How many houses or cars do we need to compensate for heart attacks or depression?

## More with less: More life energy with less money

Joe Dominguez and Vicki Robin make a wonderful breakthrough in thinking about money and life satisfaction in their bestseller, *Your Money or Your Life*.[2] Their key insight is that "money is something we trade our life energy for."

In earning money, we sell our time, which is really our "life energy." The effort to make a living consumes our life.

We underestimate how much life energy is being consumed by our work. We overestimate what we are getting in return. That's a bad bargain, as Dominguez and Robin point out:

> Are you working for less than you're worth and bringing home less money than you need? Or are you earning far more than you need for fulfillment? What is the purpose of that extra money? If it serves no purpose, would you want to work less and have more time to do what matters to you? If it does serve a purpose, is it so clear and so connected with your values that it brings joy to your hours at work? If not, what needs to change?...

> When you break the link between work and money, you give yourself the opportunity to discover what your true work is — it may turn out to be totally unrelated to what you are currently doing for money.

The 80/20 Way offers *more life energy for less effort*:

❏ Through saving and accumulating money, we avoid trading our life energy for money. With enough investment income, we can stop depleting our life energy through unfulfilling work. We choose our work and our hours. By doing what is important to us and what we enjoy, we multiply our life energy.

❏ We might decide to use savings to subsidize our ideal life-and work-style. Maybe work six months a year, then travel round the world or undertake a project with our family. Or work three days a week, routinely enjoying long weekends. We might take a pay cut and work where we want, or become our own boss.

Instead of money ruling our lives, making work stressful or miserable, we can use money to regain control of life. We can deploy energy where we're most carefree, creative, and content.

Use time and money *intelligently*. Make less go further. The quality and value of time soar once we control them.

"Success" can be self-defeating. We sacrifice our independence and time to make money, believing that more money will make us happier. It doesn't. All we do is squander our life energy at ever-higher levels of affluence.

The 80/20 Way breaks the logjam. However much or little we earn, we save, invest, and multiply money. We are less concerned about our careers than with enjoying our work. When we have built up substantial savings, they feed our independence. We spend our life on the things we care most about.

# The 80/20 Way to benefit from money

## *Step 1: Focus on your 80/20 destination*

Writing down your ideal destination works wonders.

Of Yale's 1953 graduating class, only 3 percent set written financial goals — similar to our 80/20 destination. Twenty years later, researchers discovered that these 3 percent had more money than all the other 97 percent!

Write down your 80/20 destination today! Is it:

- ❏ **To be free of money worries?**

- ❏ **To be able to afford to do the work you want and live the life you want?**

- ❏ **To have enough to be able to buy a home?**

- ❏ **To give up needing two pay checks to live?**

- ❏ **To be financially independent at a certain age, able to live off your investment income without needing to work for money?**

- ❏ **To become a millionaire?**

- ❏ **Some other objective?**

Is your 80/20 destination extremely important to you? Why?

Money is a means, not an end. Money is for freedom, not slavery; for security, not worry. Unless money is used to give you greater freedom and happiness, accumulating money is a burden.

Be specific. You want to be free of money worries? Fine, but what does this mean? Enough to live with no income for six months? Two years? Having a particular sum of money in the bank?

You'd greatly prefer another job that pays less? Fine. What's the job? What does it pay? What would your monthly expenses be? The good news is, they may be much lower — perhaps because of less expensive work clothes, lower commuting costs, or the ability to live in a less expensive area.

Helen and James are lawyers in their late twenties. They met at work, fell in love, and got married. They work for a high-powered law firm, Bullie Brake & Desmay, and are moving up the ranks. The only problem is that they hate the work and the firm.

The 80/20 destination for Helen and James is to leave the firm and start a family. Helen will retire. James wants to work for a legal advice charity, even though it pays much less. How are they going to get there?

## Step 2: Find the 80/20 route

Because of compound interest, money becomes concentrated in few hands. There is therefore one, and only one, infallible 80/20 route to enough money — *to save and invest in the easiest possible way*.

There are many difficult ways to save. Budgeting is one. Budgeting doesn't work because unexpected expenses always blow you off course.

Happily, there's an easy 80/20 route to saving.

### AARON TELLS THE SECRET OF EASY SAVING

"I liked the idea of making some money," Aaron tells Alison, "not to become a millionaire, but to have a deposit to buy a home of my own. That's my '80/20 destination,' as Richard calls it, where I want to go.

"But then I thought: How can I possibly save? Mum never could. Neither could I. Last year, Richard told me to save. I really tried. But by the end of the month there was nothing left, so how could I save? Then Richard said, there's an answer to that too.

"Save first, he said. Pay yourself first. That means you save 10 percent of your pay before you spend any. You save automatically. The savings go straight into a special savings account on pay day. You can't spend it, it's gone already.

"But it's the same difference, I said. If I don't have the money at the start of the month, I'll run out faster. By month end I'll be starving. But Richard said no, it's not the same, you'll see.

"He was right. I really don't miss the money. I must stretch it longer, because there's less to start with in my pocket. I couldn't believe it. Before, I was convinced I couldn't save. I've managed it for 12 months and I can carry on forever. Honest, Alison, you could do it, anyone could. You don't see the money and it's just like they taxed you more or you earned less."

Helen and James decide to stay at Bullie Brake & Desmay, save and invest 10 percent of their pay — by automatic deduction — and accumulate enough to eventually live their dream. How long will it take?

Together, Helen and James earn $6,500 a month. After tax, $4,000. Currently, they spend it all. They have no savings.

They calculate that if they moved to a cheaper area, near James's legal aid charity, they could live on $2,500 a month, even with the planned baby. The charity can only afford to pay James $2,600 a month. After tax, about $2,000. So they need $500 investment income a month — $6,000 a year — to plug the gap.

They plan to buy an apartment for $60,000 and rent it. After repairs, maintenance, and tax, they'll make $6,000 a year. So they need $60,000 savings to change their lives.

Ten percent of their annual pay is $7,800. If they invest the money at 10 percent, that's $66,000 within six years. Even at 5 percent, within a tax-exempt plan they'll accumulate nearly $67,000 by year seven.

## The basic 80/20 route to making the money you need

Save and invest 10 percent of your income before you receive it by having it automatically channeled into a savings account.

Do this as early as you can in life — which means NOW!

Frankly, this is 95 percent of the advice that anyone needs. This is the easy way to end your money worries. No other way is remotely as powerful.

## Refinements to the basic 80/20 route

Can you reach your destination faster?

- ❑ No investment is as good as paying off your credit card debt.

- ❑ The next best investment is to "retire" all your other debts. Start with the most expensive. Even though mortgage — property bond — interest rates are now very low, it's almost impossible to find an investment as attractive as paying off your mortgage, when you have the savings to do so.

- ❑ Cut up your credit cards. You're bound to spend less. If you need a card, get a debit card so you can only spend what you have in the bank.

- ❏ Be more selective in buying things. Only spend money on the few items that really make you happy. Spend more on the 20 percent that gives you 80 percent of pleasure, and less on the rest.

- ❏ Ask yourself, "Do I really enjoy this item I'm spending money on? Is it really in the 20 percent of items giving me 80 percent of satisfaction from spending?" If not, cut it out. You'll have more money for the best 20 percent of spending and more life energy too — you won't need to spend so much time earning.

- ❏ Go for cheaper items that deliver most of the benefit. A two-year-old car may be 95 percent as beneficial as a new car, at just 60 percent of the cost. Second-hand furniture may cost only 20 percent of the new price.

- ❏ With spare cash, buy assets that promise income or an increase in value: for example, any sort of land or property, art, or collectible items. Pick anything that delights you and appreciates.

- ❏ Save half any pay raise. Increase your automatic saving before it hits your bank account.

- ❏ Spring clean each year — get rid of the clutter. Give away the small items, sell the valuable ones, and invest the proceeds.

- ❏ Draw a wall chart of your monthly income and expenses. It'll encourage you to cut expenses and augment income. See Figure 10 overleaf for an example.

- ❏ Prepare a wall chart of your monthly income, expenses, and investment income, with a projection of when investment income will meet your monthly expenses. This is financial independence day: you're no longer dependent on your job for your living. Figure 11 overleaf is an illustration.

- ❏ Cut one item of spending. Give the money away. Not only is this likely to give you greater pleasure, but also, mysteriously, it often increases your income.

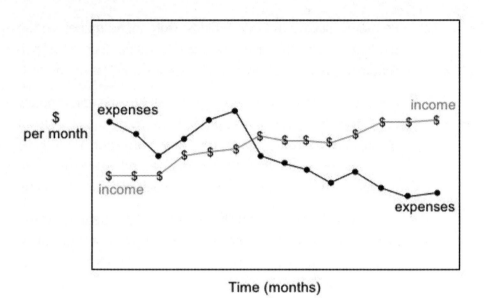

Figure 10  Elizabeth's wall chart of monthly income and expenses

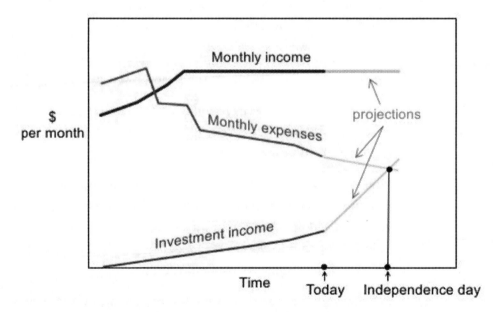

Figure 11  Donna's financial independence wall chart

## Is compound interest different from investment?

Compound interest is hugely powerful, but only works for you once you've saved and invested, in a high-interest savings account, or investments like bonds, property, or other assets that will likely appreciate. Be careful with bank accounts — banks often rip off unwary customers, and many so-called "high-interest" accounts are anything but.

## What rate of investment return is realistic?

My examples assume a 5–10 percent annual investment return. Two words of caution, however. First, you must try to avoid tax. Most countries have special tax-free accounts for small savers and investors, but you must be careful to put your investments in these accounts.

Second, we're at a time when inflation and interest rates in many places are at 50-year lows. This makes it necessary to shop around, even to get a 5 percent return. The highest bank accounts may pay only 3–4 percent. Other forms of low-risk investment may be necessary.

## Where should you invest?

The basic objective is to make at least 5 percent long-term annual return at minimum risk.

- ❑ First, pay off all your debt.

- ❑ Invest in risk-free savings accounts if they pay interest at 5 percent or greater.

- ❑ You may be able to invest in "bonds" — government or company debt — that "yields" (pays interest) more than 5 percent.

- ❑ Long-term, direct investment in suitable property — maybe your home — is attractive. Long-run property prices — really the price of the land beneath the property — have risen about 8 percent a year. The supply of land is fixed, yet demand tends to rise, driven by demand for larger houses, second houses, and a falling number of people per household. Where population and wealth are increasing — for example, most attractive and warm parts of the United States or Southern Europe, or expanding cities anywhere — land is a good long-term bet.

❑ Be chary of the stock market. It may fall and fall. If you have enough money to invest, consider a "market-neutral hedge fund," one not affected by general stock market fluctuations. Hedge funds may be lower risk and more attractive than traditional "mutual funds," which depend on rising stock markets.

❑ Shun anything — shares, property, or the latest hot trend — with recent sharp appreciation. Bubbles burst. Wait until prices fall and then stabilize. Never buy in a market that is rising or falling fast. In the short term, stick to safe investments even if you can only get 5 percent.

❑ Should you start your own business? Most millionaires become rich by starting a venture. But beware. Only one in twenty new businesses succeeds. Probably 99 percent of the payoff comes from 1 percent of the new ventures. Will you really be in the lucky 1 percent?

❑ Only invest in a new venture if you also have savings to fall back on. Don't risk losing everything. If you won't sleep at night, don't invest. Becoming mega-rich probably won't make you happy anyway. It's a very bad gamble.

❑ If you're passionate about starting your business, wait until you have cash that you can afford to lose. Or go for a low-risk venture that requires little capital — for example, a stall in the neighborhood market, a service business like mowing lawns or cleaning cars, or a delivery service using your own car.

## *Step 3: Take 80/20 action NOW!*

You're at a crossroads.

You can go ahead and instruct your bank to deduct 10 percent of your monthly income and put it into a savings account. You can then look forward to a life without money worries, to your 80/20 destination.

Or you can do nothing.

Go ahead. Do it now. It takes five minutes to arrange. The benefit, for the rest of your life, will be enormous. Make friends with money — boost your life energy immeasurably!

Imagine you've freed yourself from money worries, perhaps even accumulated a small fortune. How is it going to make you happier? How far will your new-found riches deepen and improve your friendships and relationships, which, as we're about to see, add the most joy to life? Money and material preoccupations pale into the background when we create and experience the bonds of true love and affection.

# Relationships the 80/20 Way

Each person kills the thing they love
Throughout the modern world,
Money and work both count above
Loved ones, who come in third.

**Modern parody of Oscar Wilde**

The project was going brilliantly. From absolutely nothing, the developer had created paradise on earth: a cornucopia of lush gardens, flowing streams, palm trees, trees of every imaginable fruit, exotic birds, dogs, cats, horses, donkeys, even a troop of tame monkeys. Multicolored mountains framed the garden. In the distance, Adam could glimpse blue sea. After taking possession, he meandered through the grounds, greeting the animals, giving them names, tasting the fruit, alternating between the warm sunshine and the shade of the trees. For the first time in his life, he felt totally secure, relaxed, and happy. He had made it.

The developer popped round for a cup of coffee the next morning.

"Do you like it?" he asked.

"Yes," Adam said, "it's fabulous. You really have done a fantastic job. The villa and the courtyard are perfect. The gardens are gorgeous. Yet, I have the feeling that something's missing. Can't quite put my finger on it though."

"Ah," said the developer. "I was thinking about it last night. You're absolutely correct and I can put it right."

"What do you have in mind?" Adam asked.

"How about," the developer said, "someone to love?"

## Or the twenty-first-century version...

The Lord God had planted a garden in Eden and there he put the man he had formed. A river watering the garden flowed from Eden. The Lord God put the man in the garden, to take care of it. And the Lord God said, "You will rule over the fish and the birds and every living creature, and be responsible for looking after them all, for your benefit, and you may eat them, provided that they continue to grow and multiply."

God saw all that he had made and it was very good. And the man agreed.

The next day, the Lord God said to the man, "It is not good for you to be alone. I will make a woman so that you can love her, have a family, and enjoy living together and raising children."

But the man said to the Lord God, "Make up your mind, O Lord. First you tell me I must be responsible for gardening, and animal husbandry, and for restocking the fish of the sea and the birds of the air, and for our general environmental policy, as well as my own hunting, fishing, and cooking. All that's a full-time job. Don't get me wrong. I love my work, it's very rewarding, and the garden is idyllic. But how do you expect me to have time for all this stuff about love and family and relationships? I can see it all getting too complicated. Let's keep it just you and me — and all the birds of the air and etcetera — right?"

And the Lord God scratched his head, and wondered what the world had come to.

There's only one happiness in life," wrote George Sand, "to love and be loved."

Carl Gustav Jung, the great psychologist, said, "We need other people to be truly ourselves." We make sense of life through relationships.

But here's the twist. Modern life is making it more and more difficult to find, nurture, and sustain love and relationships. Perhaps without realizing it, certainly without resisting it, most of us are opting for a higher quantity of lower-quality relationships. We have more relationships, but they mean less. And our romantic relationship is ever more endangered or elusive.

We all know that urgent work obligations and modern technology such as personal computers, emails, and cellular phones are eating into family life. The trend is most pronounced in the United States. Twenty years ago, half of all married Americans claimed that "our whole family usually eats together"; now that proportion is down to a third. More women are working, fewer people are married, married people have fewer children, the number of unmarried mothers has increased, our desire for large families has slumped, divorce rates have climbed, and the time that parents and children spend together has plummeted.

The trends reflect increased economic pressures and the insidious prevalence of monetary concerns. Like all other fixed costs, families — and the number of children in them — are being downsized.

Following the business trend, more and more families are "outsourcing" more and more activities — babysitting, childminding, food preparation, cooking, cleaning, gardening, organizing kids' birthday parties, care of the sick and elderly — that were previously knit into the fabric of family relationships.

More families need two workers to sustain their living standards. For those in the fast lane, work for both partners is more demanding and difficult to square with traditional family responsibilities.

## BOB AND JANE

Meet my good friends, Bob and Jane. Both fun people, they lead a hectic lifestyle, globetrotting for work. When I met them, they had two delightful girls — Emma, 9, and Anne, 11 — a decorous if demanding dog, and two large houses. Both helped to run the household. Most friends were friends of both Jane and Bob. When Jane had a project in Brazil for three months, she took the children, and Bob visited for a week's holiday and odd weekends. It seemed to work, but I became concerned about the stress imposed by different demands on their time. Might they drift apart?

Eight years later they are divorced — still friends, but bruised and regretful. Are they happier apart? I doubt it. They had a great relationship, supporting each other and their children. Could it have been different?

I can't be sure. But I suspect that with less intense work pressures — in the 1960s, or if they had followed the 80/20 Way today — they would have stuck together, and at least four people would have been happier.

## Do more relationships add to happiness?

Carnegie Mellon University researchers studied 169 randomly selected local people for two years, tracking their use of the internet and its effect on happiness and relationships. Sponsored by computer and software companies, the researchers were confident that the greater variety and richness of relationships established over the web would decrease social isolation and increase wellbeing.

Both sponsors and researchers were startled and disconcerted by the results. The more internet relationships were established and the more time spent on the web, the more lonely and depressed people tended to become. True, email and chat rooms increased the quantity of relation-ships, but these were shallow; and the time spent on them detracted from more important relationships with family and friends. Intensive, face-to-face contact with a few people turns out to be essential for security and happiness. Less is more.

The trend toward *more but less rich* relationships is most acute for the (apparent) winners today. Money rich but time poor, and great believers in the market, they buy relationships there. I don't mean that they use prostitutes; although it's remarkable that many of my acquaintances who suddenly become rich immediately suffer marital difficulties, not entirely unrelated to their strings of affairs. (With more money, they want more relationships, not realizing that more is less.)

What I do mean is that the winners contract relationships with a bewildering array of professional service purveyors: personal trainers, personal assistants, personal coaches, pedicurists, shrinks, massage therapists, food consultants, hypnotists, aromatherapists, tennis coaches, communications advisers, spiritual guides, and God knows who else.

"Be good to yourself," they say. The marketing patter is working. Between 1990 and 2000, for example, the number of personal trainers in the United States doubled, to over 100,000. When I was a management consultant, my firm focused very much on the personal relationship with the chief executive officer, and prospered accordingly.

Successful people may have little time for life at home, so they buy attention in bite-sized chunks, conveniently packaged to fit the executive agenda. The army of household assistants take care of the family, while the personal service providers pamper the breadwinners.

It's all a ghastly mistake. Certainly each professional service provides something of value, but more is less — these commercial relationships substitute for the primary relationships that are essential for happiness.

The professionals win; everyone else loses.

**W**hy is *more* affluence not translating into *more* happiness? Why does prosperity corrode personal and social relationships? It's not the wealth itself — all other things being equal, increased comfort, healthcare, and knowledge should raise human freedom and security, and perhaps also generosity. It's down to the way we think and act.

We're becoming utterly transfixed by one obsession — *more with more*. We want more money, more goods, more friends, more relationships, more sex, more attention, more comfort, more houses, more travel, more gadgets, and more public acknowledgment. We are prepared to pay dearly for these aspirations. We worry more and spend more time, more attention, more energy — and, frankly, more of our souls and ourselves — to work to invest or pay for more stuff.

Yet the economy works well because it follows a different principle, that of more with less. Economic life is a constant quest for more with less: better, faster, and yet cheaper goods and services. Less is made more.

Human happiness — like true personal success — is immutably driven by the same laws: less is more, and more with less. There is an unavoidable tradeoff between quality and quantity. *More* means *worse*. It is only by focusing on what is genuinely important to us — the few people, relationships, activities, and causes that we really care about — that we become centered, authentic, powerful, loving, and loved. There is no other way.

The way to enjoy more with less in relationships and life is plain:

❑ Create more with less in your work life, gaining more money and enjoyment with less time, without eating into your family and personal life.

❑ Gain more with less by saving, so that sooner or later you will have the investment income to pay for the lifestyle you want and are not dependent on an ultra-demanding job.

❑ Focus on less is more: what is important for your happiness — satisfying work, a sense of personal purpose, and above all a few high-quality relationships — which require, and will amply repay, unstinting time and emotional commitment.

## Quality versus quantity

Almost certainly, 80 percent of the satisfaction from our relationships flows from 20 percent or fewer of the relationships.

> *Good news*: We can focus attention on a few key relationships; we don't have to worry about the unimportant relationships.

> *Action to hike happiness*: Put most time, energy, attention, creativity, and imagination into our few most important relationships.

Ask what proportion of that effort goes into your most important relationships, the few that deliver most of your satisfaction. Probably, these 20 percent of key relationships take more than 20 percent of the energy you devote to relationships. How much more? 40 percent? 60 percent? Unless you are devoting at least 80 percent of your "relationship energy" to the 20 percent of key relationships, you can increase your happiness by doing so.

> *Good news*: Satisfaction can soar even without increasing the total amount of "relationship energy," simply by focusing energy on key relationships.

> *Action to hike happiness*: Redirect energy so that at least 80 percent of "relationship energy" goes into your few key relationships.

Why do telephone companies everywhere around the globe give us seven-digit phone numbers? Because we can remember a sequence of seven numbers, but not eight or nine.

We can only care deeply about a few people. Unless we limit the number of people who are central to our lives, nobody will be.

The ultimate tradeoff between quantity and quality comes with the one relationship that can be central to our happiness.

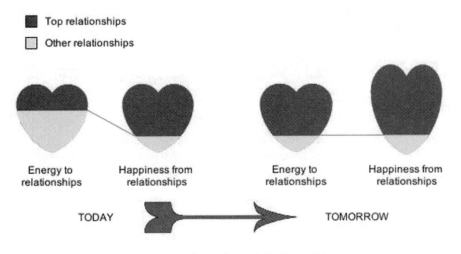

**Figure 11 Moving energy into key relationships**

## Someone to love

A recent study by psychologists Diener and Seligman found that, with only one exception, *everyone* in their top 10 percent of extremely happy people was in a romantic relationship. Another revealing fact is that 40 percent of married Americans say that they are "extremely happy," while only 23 percent of Americans who have not yet married claim the same. Finding the right partner is a ticket to happiness for many people.

Yet the time, effort, and intelligence that we devote to finding a mate is often very limited.

Harvard professor George Zipf showed that 70 percent of the marriages he studied in Philadelphia in 1931 were between people who lived within just a few blocks of each other, within 30 percent of the area he studied. The whole of Philadelphia was too big a place for most residents to trawl for love. As for looking out of town, forget it!

Most romances still spring from the local neighborhood, a small circle of friends, or colleagues at work. And many people follow the "bus stop" approach to love. They take the first lover who comes along.

They fall

# in love

# *with love.*

Love at first sight usually doesn't work. Committing to a life partner based largely on sexual attraction and performance in bed is a poor bet. Sex is wonderful, but sooner or later the appeal will pall. A long-term relationship needs more.

True love — mutual admiration for each other and excitement — can move mountains and make even the most unlikely relationship work. But romantic love may not last. To be happy over the long haul, consider four wider qualities.

## *Being able to get close to other people, depend on them, and have them depend on you*

There are three sorts of people:

- ❑  *Secure* people, for whom intimacy and dependence are easy.

- ❑  Those who *avoid* commitment and intimacy — when care is needed, they run for the sidelines.

- ❑  *Anxious* people, who are uncertain of love and dispense care compulsively, all the time — whether their lover wants it or not.

A few minutes' reflection should reveal which type you and any potential partner are.[1] With two secure individuals, the prospects for a successful relationship are very good. If only one individual is secure, the odds are far less favorable, but still reasonable. If neither person is secure, the chances are poor.

If you are not secure yourself, to be happy in the long term you *must* select a secure partner.

## *Being optimistic*

Do you and your prospective mate search for the silver lining or the cloud? When things are going wrong, optimists look for temporary or specific explanations — "the boss was in a foul mood" or "I was up half last night." Pessimists assume deep-seated, permanent problems — "I'm not good at my job," "that problem won't go away."

Choose an optimistic partner, or one willing to learn optimism; it can be learned.[2]

## *Ability to avoid harsh argument and criticism of partner*

Professor John Gottman uses a "love lab" to observe the behavior of partners. Nine times out of ten, he correctly predicts divorce.

Gottman's danger signals are frequent fierce arguments, criticizing the mate in personal terms, showing contempt, being chilly or withdrawn, and being unable to take criticism.

Ensure that you have a trial period in which the two of you get closer without final commitment. If you experience Gottman's signals, walk.

## *Agreement on basic values*

Select someone who has the same basic values on fundamental issues, such as honesty, money, kindness, or whatever's crucial to you.

C hoose your lover after deep deliberation. Don't drift into a relationship. Search far and wide for the right person. Know the few qualities that you most want in a partner. Experiment. Test whether the relationship *really* works before you fully commit. Take your time. There are many stages and gradations of commitment — don't rush them. An increasing sense of certainty should develop naturally.

Any relationship only has a few vital requirements. Often we don't enquire closely enough what these are, so we act randomly, frittering away most of our energy on actions that lead nowhere.

> *Good news*: Focusing on the few things that matter makes all the difference between success and failure in relationships.

> *Action to hike happiness*: In each key relationship, identify the few actions that lead to the greatest happiness. Concentrate your effort on them.

A wise friend once told me:

> We are all different and things that are not important to me are often very important to my wife, and the other way round.
>
> In our marriage, this is what really matters to her. She wants me to be home on time. She wants to always be able to rely on me. She loves flowers. She loves me supporting her in her projects. She adores surprises.
>
> These are not necessarily the things that I would most want to do for her. I could take her to candlelit dinners, I could buy her the car I'd like myself, take her on great vacations, I could do all sorts of other things, but nothing would impress her if I haven't met the basic few needs that mean most to her.

Don't do for others what you would like yourself. Do what *your partner* wants.

Another couple has many marital problems. In a candid moment, the wife confided, "What Peter doesn't realize is that if he just brought me home a bunch of flowers every week or two, I would do anything for him."

How sad and unnecessary: so little effort of the right type required, such a huge reward. How many marriages are barren, loveless places because the simple needs of a partner are not being met? And yet, the springs of love could easily be unstopped and overflow again.

## Happy families

Just before South America was conquered, the Indians in Peru spotted Spanish sailing ships on the horizon. Not knowing what a ship looked like, they didn't realize that these could contain soldiers. Assuming that the boats were a freak of the weather, the Indians ignored the warning.

We also deprive ourselves of vital knowledge if we don't know what to look for. Our relationships aren't only romantic ones, the people who are important to us obviously include our children. Those of us who didn't have a particularly happy childhood often repeat the sad pattern as parents, because we don't know how happy families work.

# Happy families are all *alike*;

every *unhappy* family is unhappy

in its own way.

*Tolstoy's* Anna Karenina

There is a formula for happy families that we can copy.

## Happy families practice "love spirals"

Most parents love their children, but in happy families the parents *demonstrate* their love all the time.

Raising children is difficult. The intensity of family life is such that things can only go two ways.

One is a downward spiral. The baby screams, the kids break something, some mishap occurs. The stressed parents respond with criticism or punishment. The kids scream louder. Things get worse and worse.

The other is an upward spiral. The kids are cute, adventurous, smiling. They love learning and attention. Even a mother's mere presence makes a young child feel secure and happy. Parents take pride in their children and practice small acts of love, which make the children even more playful and sunny. This in turn elicits further love from the parents, and so on.

Both spirals are evident in all families, yet in happy families the positive spirals outweigh the negative ones. Over time, the children in happy families become more secure and content and will usually reinforce the positive spirals.

The parents set the tone by their early actions, when the family is just starting and the first baby is born. By creating and reinforcing the positive spirals and defusing the negative ones, the parents slowly but surely craft a happy family.

The return on early acts of parental love is enormous. For relatively little effort, there is a massive benefit, for the child and the whole family.

## Happy families use more positive than negative feedback

Researchers at one school noticed that teachers praised good work and blamed bad behavior. As an experiment, teachers were trained to praise both good work and good behavior — and to ignore bad behavior. Soon the bad behavior largely vanished.

At home, too, praise is more effective than blame, creating upward spirals. The 80/20 Way exalts praise — praise is easy and the return over the lifetime of the child is immense. Praise is to children's development as water is to plants: the tiniest encouragement leads to massive flowering. A capable, well-intentioned child will have a terrific positive impact on other people throughout life. A little praise for a child today has enormous lasting benefits.

Try counting the number of times you and your spouse say "yes" or "no" to your children. Make a conscious effort to say "yes" more and "no" less. Count again a week later. See the difference it makes.

## Happy families have parents who are always available and generous with their time

Close bonding between parent and child creates security and happiness throughout life.

Children don't understand the concept of "quality time," they want attention *all* the time. They are right. The 80/20 Way is to give *more care and love to fewer people*, the people we care most about. All time spent with one of your children is time well spent, with an enormous payoff for the child, for the rest of the family, and for society.

If you really can't be available for your children, make sure that you are elsewhere or invisible — absence can be accepted, being too busy when you are visible cannot.

## Happy families have united and loving parents

Children are shrewd, skilled negotiators. They love playing off one parent against the other. They find conflict intriguing and sometimes empowering.

At all costs, quash such games. Parents need to show that they love one another, even when they are annoyed. The payoff is that forcing love to win over grumpiness will make you happier too.

## *Happy families can cope with disaster or difficult children*

Happy families, by and large, do not have an easier time than unhappy families. They just cope better with challenges.

If you have children, be prepared for the *possibility* of a difficult child. Children are unpredictable free agents and they can shock you.

Some friends had a very difficult son, yet coped with him very well. I asked them how.

"We went for parent effectiveness training," said the father. "They divide problems into three categories. There are our own problems, caused by the parents or the rest of the family. Then there are shared problems, created by child and family together. Then there are the child's own problems, essentially unrelated to the family. Each type requires a different solution."

"When we were counseled," his wife added, "we found that most of the conflict flowed from our son's problems. We were trained to change our response, when Charles [the son] had problems. We offered suggestions to him and left it to him to decide what he was going to do. This reduced family conflict by three-quarters; our family life became far happier. Charles was happier, because we stopped telling him what to do all the time."

## *Happy families impose discipline but never withdraw love*

Punishment works, but only when the limits of acceptable behavior are completely clear, so the child knows what he or she is being punished for. Withdrawing privileges for a time is safe and effective. It must always be clear that the punishment is for the action and isn't a reflection on the child's character. Whatever the child has done, never suspend warmth, affection, or love.

Some very good friends learnt this the hard way. They have two boys, now in their late teens, both intelligent and charming. Over the years, however, they have had major problems with Daniel, the younger child.

When he was 11, Daniel stole some money and successfully — for a time — deflected the blame onto an innocent schoolmate. Daniel's mother, feeling that radical action was necessary, withdrew her affection from Daniel — for a month, she refused to talk to him or have anything to do with him.

Her action proved disastrous. When she realized her mistake, she tried to make up for it by very close love, attention, and constructive action over the next five years. But Daniel, and therefore the whole family, continued to have significant problems, partly caused by the withdrawal of love at that very difficult time.

Punishment is not the only, nor usually the best, way of imposing discipline. When faced with a crying, pouting, or demanding child, it's tempting to punish or give way to the kid's demands for the sake of peace. Instead, however, the child can be told that whining won't work, but that a "smiley face" might do the trick. If from the age of four you reward smiley faces more than screams and pouts, guess what your child will tend to go for?

## Happy families share bedtime stories and "best moments"

The 10–20 minutes before children fall asleep are the most priceless and influential. Reading a suitable story demonstrates love and sends the child off to sleep with a store of dreaming material.

One friend's kids love their bedtime stories, because dad makes up stories that include them as key characters. You can work out the stories in advance or ask imaginative friends for ideas.

Another great idea is to ask your children, "What did you like doing today?" If they remember all the good things, they will go to sleep in a peaceful and satisfied frame of mind. Some psychologists believe that this practice helps to inoculate children against depression.

Given the value of this time, both to the children directly and in cementing your bond with them, make this a daily habit. The effort is small — the reward enormous.

## Friends

Aside from family, whose death would leave you desolated? Count those people. Those are your key friends, the 20 percent who contribute 80 percent of meaning and value to you.

Most people come up with 10 or fewer names, although they usually know 100 or 200 people. My address book lists 207 friends, but only 18 of these are truly significant to me. These friends are less than 9 percent of the total, yet give me at least 90 percent of "friendship pleasure."

Work out how much time you spend with your key friends and with other friends. You may be surprised. You're more likely to spend time with neighbors whom you like moderately than with your best friends if they're in a distant town. You'd probably be happier the other way round.

Try to live near your best friends. In any case, see them frequently.

## The 80/20 Way to greater love

### Step 1: Focus on your 80/20 destination

As you answer the questions opposite, remember that less is more — be more selective and focus in depth on what truly matters in your life.

## MY 80/20 DESTINATION FOR GREATER LOVE

1    Do I want and need to find a lover?

2    Do I want to make a specific person my lover?

3    Do I need to do things differently to be sure of keeping my lover?

4    Do I want a happy family? Am I ready for the commitment and actions needed to raise happy children?

5    Do I want to see my best friends more often?

## *Step 2: Find the 80/20 route*

How can you obtain more with less — deeper commitment and love, with less angst and striving?

---

MY 80/20 ROUTE TO GREATER LOVE

1   If I don't have a lover to whom I'm fully committed, what type of person do I want to love for the long haul:

Do I want a secure person?

Do I want an optimistic person?

Do I want someone who can avoid harsh personal criticism and frequent arguments?

Do I want someone who agrees with my basic values? What are these?


2   Do I know anyone I might want as my lover?

Are they secure?

Are they optimistic?

Are they able to avoid harsh criticism and arguments?

Do they share my basic values?

---

3    Where am I most likely to find the right lover?

What actions could I take to meet him or her?

Which actions would give me the best result for my energy and which would I enjoy most?

4    Do I know the few things that will keep my lover happy? (Try asking!)

What are the few actions I need to take every day or week to deliver on my lover's key needs?

5    Can I raise a happy family?

Can I practice love spirals?

Can I give much more positive than negative feedback?

Can I be available for my children and generous with my time?

Are my partner and I united and loving?

Could I cope with disaster or difficult children and keep being loving?

Can I impose standards but never withdraw love?

Do I spend the last 15 minutes of each child's day with them?

6    If I want to see my best friends more often, how am I going to arrange this?

Which route gives me the best solution for the least effort and expense?

## Step 3: Take 80/20 action

---

80/20 ACTION FOR GREATER LOVE

What are the three most important actions that I should take now?

     Action 1:


     Action 2:


     Action 3:


Where can I take energy away from superficial or unimportant relationships to use on my three key actions?

---

Modern norms are out of kilter with our deepest needs for love and affection. In pursuit of more with more, many of society's most "successful" people are putting their jobs and careers first, and trying to fill the emotional hole that this creates by expanding the number and variety of relationships that they enjoy. Inevitably, most of these relationships are superficial and unsatisfying. In devoting energy to a large number of relationships and to work, they deprive themselves of the meaning and joy that flow from a few central relationships and one love affair.

In relationships, above all, less is more.

# The 8 Simple, Good Life

The ability to simplify means to eliminate the unnecessary, so
that the necessary may speak.

artist Hans Hofmann

Thinking about lunch, the vacationing businessman stared
at the calm, blue sea. A small boat, laden with large
yellow-fin tuna, docked near the pretty Mexican village. A lone fisherman
jumped ashore.

"That's a great catch," said the tourist. "How long did it take you?"

"Not so long," replied the Mexican.

"Why didn't you stay out longer and catch more fish?"

"That's enough to keep the family provided for."

"What do you do with the rest of your time?"

"Sleep late, fish a little, play with my children, have lunch, take a siesta
with Maria, my wife. Stroll into the village each evening, sip wine, play
guitar and cards with my amigos — a full and rich life, señor."

"I think I could help you," the visitor said, wrinkling his nose. "I'm a
Harvard MBA and this is the advice you'd get at business school. Spend
more time fishing, buy a bigger boat, make more money, then several
boats until you've got a fleet. Don't sell the catch to a middleman, sell
directly to the processor, eventually opening your own cannery. You'd
control the product, production, and distribution. You could then leave
this small town behind, move to Mexico City, then Los Angeles, perhaps
eventually to New York City to run your expanding firm."

"But señor, how long would this take?"

"Fifteen, twenty years."

"But what then, señor?"

"That's the best part," the businessman laughed. "When the time is right, you could float on the stock market and make millions of dollars."

"Hmm, millions you say. What then, señor?"

"Then you could retire and go home. Move to a pretty village by the sea, sleep late, fish a little, play with your kids, take a siesta with your wife, stroll to the village evenings, sip wine, and play guitar and cards with your friends."

## What is the good life?

Three centuries before Christ, Greek philosophers debated what made the good life. Perhaps the most convincing view came from Epicurus, who took his own advice and lived very happily.

"I don't know how I could imagine the good life," he said, "if I take away the pleasure of taste, if I take away sexual pleasure, the pleasure of hearing, or the sweet emotions caused by seeing beautiful forms."

Epicurus said that all we need for happiness is:

❏   **Food, shelter, clothes**

❏   **Friends**

❏   **Freedom**

❏   **Thought**

"To live one's entire life in happiness," he said, "the greatest by far is the possession of friendship... a handful of true friends." He took a house outside Athens and moved in with seven friends. "Never eat alone," he advised, "eating with friends is much better."

Epicurus' circle valued freedom. To avoid unpleasant work, they formed a commune. They grew cabbages, onions, and artichokes, and relished their independence. They exchanged ideas and wrote books. Life was simple, far from lavish, but fully satisfying. "Luxurious food and drinks," Epicurus said, "do not produce freedom from harm or a healthy condition. We must regard wealth beyond what is natural as no more use than water to a container that is full to overflowing."

Epicurus and his friends believed that *less is more*. Contrast this with the modern *more with more* compulsion. A recent survey of AOL subscribers asked how much more money they would need for them to be free of worrying about money. It turned out that those with incomes over $100,000 thought they needed far more money than those with incomes under $40,000. The high earners were five times more likely to say they needed at least another $90,000 annual income. This should tell us that once we pursue more with more, we can never, ever win, never be satisfied.

It is not innate greed that propels us toward wanting more with more. It is the structure of modern life and its compelling, insidious assumptions. Modern life insists that success is a matter of more money, that more money means more work, that there is only a fast track and a slow track, and that the fast track requires us to lay out huge effort for huge rewards. We worry about how we're doing, we work more than we want, we buy more than we can value, and we cut ourselves off from the simple joys of romantic love, family, friends, and abundant time.

But what if it really *is* possible to get more with less? Then we can experience the marvelous parts of modern life — the challenge of exciting work, the discovery of our talents, material plenty — while also relishing control of our time and rich personal relationships. We square the circle by focusing on our high-value activities — those of high value to other people and to ourselves — and cutting out the trivial ones. We simplify, we purify, we intensify, and we relax, all at once.

More with more is like the emperor's new clothes. Everyone professes that this is the way to live, although nobody who searches their own soul can really see the point. We are all swept along by near-total unanimity that the emperor's outfit is magnificent. Yet within each of us lurks the ability, at any moment, to blurt out what we really know and feel: that the emperor is in the altogether. More with more leads to less fraternity and happiness; more with less leads to a life of higher quality, worth, and deep personal satisfaction.

Since the pursuit of more with less runs counter to modern life, we must make a deliberate decision to step off the more with more treadmill. Why does this seem so difficult?

There are perhaps three reasons:

- ❏ Our desires are infinite and contradictory. We are restless, ambitious, and conditioned to think that more is better.

- ❏ We compare ourselves to other people. As some friends become richer, we don't want to fall behind. If the neighbors have a new car, I want one too, even though I'm perfectly happy with the old one. Even if I'm lucky enough to own a yacht, I'll notice that the owner of the next berth has just bought a bigger one with more powerful radar.

- ❏ Many of us believe that ambition, effort, and striving are good, that we must develop our abilities and reach for the stars. We feel guilty if we are not competing, struggling to go further.

You can leave the treadmill with a light heart, however, since:

- ❏ The vast majority of our desires don't lead to more than fleeting happiness. To be happy we need to focus our demands, boiling them down to the few that are *most important* to us and result in our happiness. When other desires come along we exclude them, not because they are the work of the devil, but because we know they won't make us happy. We stop worrying. We simplify.

❑    Comparing our goods to the neighbors' is as old as humanity
— Adam and Eve surely compared their fig leaves, and Moses'
tenth commandment forbade hankering after the neighbor's
house, wife, houseboy, au pair, ox, or ass — but the consumer
society raises the temptation to an art form. The advertising
and marketing industry has rendered us addicted to joyless
comparison and acquisition of goods — our economy revolves
around the pointless, never-ending race for more.

If we must compare ourselves to our neighbor, is it better
to compare relative wealth or happiness? Moses should have
said, "Come on friends, covet anything you like, but realize
that it's been scientifically proven that possessions don't lead
to happiness. Now, would you rather have lots of houses,
slaves, and cattle, or be happy?"

Do you have too few possessions or too many? Would your
long-term happiness be greater if you added complexity or if
you simplified? Do you use all your possessions? For one
answer, look in your closets — have you simplified your
wardrobe to the point where it contains only clothes you wear
frequently, or is it stuffed with the 80 percent of clothes you
wear less than 20 percent of the time?

❑    Stretching and cultivating ourselves is good: we become happier, more individual, and more use to other people. But striving to the point that we're stressed out, time poor, snappy,
and unhappy is stupid. We do more good when we are
relaxed and focused. We add most to the happiness of those
we love when we are happy ourselves. We are happiest when
we simplify our lives down to the essentials that work best for
us.

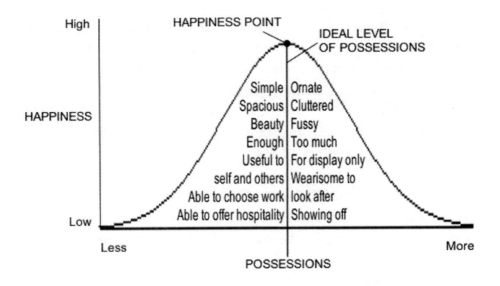

Figure 13  The happiness point for possessions

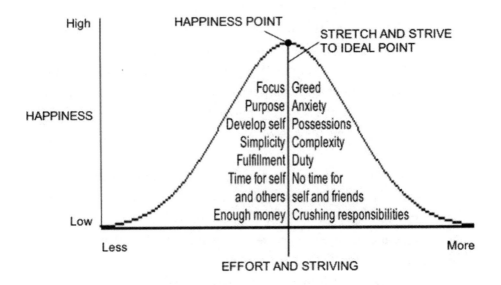

Figure 14  The happiness point for effort and striving

The happiness point is the degree of effort and striving that makes us happiest in the long term. Where are you on the curve? Would you be happier and more developed with more striving, or with less?

To jump off the treadmill requires a clean break — decisive action to reject the worries and complexity of modern life, crafting instead our own simple, good life, confident that we can create more with less.


## ANN FINDS THE SIMPLE, GOOD LIFE

Ann's a close friend. In her twenties, she was a successful account executive in advertising. At 29, she made an abrupt shift. She quit her job and has never had another. For 10 years she's simplified her life down to the things she wants to do, creative activities of one kind or another.

"I was having fun in advertising," she told me, "and making good money. One day I sat down and asked myself what I really wanted to do with my life. The answer was clear. I wanted to paint, to sculpt, to write music and play the piano. Learn how to play other instruments. Pursue my own projects.

"I didn't want to climb the corporate ladder, get stuck in traffic to and from the office, work for a boss, run the rat race. Better to work at home, control my time, be free to walk in the sunshine, see a friend. Above all, develop my creative side, see where that took me.

"I moved out of my big house. Bought a one-room, pretty studio, with a great mezzanine floor beneath a skylight. Parents went nuts, especially Dad. They'd made sacrifices so I could go to university, were very proud of my progress, my lifestyle. Didn't understand I had to follow my own path, didn't want to die rich but with the music still inside me. Kept asking me where the money was going to come from.

"A good question. When I'd earned good money, I spent a lot. Had some savings but they went for the deposit on my studio. But I soon found that I didn't need to spend much. No expenses going to work, didn't need my flash sports car, expensive clothes to impress clients. No need to eat in fancy restaurants. The first year after I quit regular work, I made only a third of what I had before. But I paid very little tax, found I could live by selling portraits and sculptures of individuals and families. The point was — I only did the things I wanted to, I was very much happier.

"I tried various ways of making money, but on one condition — that I had to enjoy it and express myself at the same time. The weird thing is that in the past five years I have begun to make good money again too, while self-employed and doing precisely what I choose."

## How to leave the more with more treadmill

Resolving to seek more with less is difficult, because we have to shake off all the erroneous assumptions of modern life. However, having made the commitment to less is more, the process of finding it is not that hard.

Why? It's a process of subtraction. We don't need to do more — we need to do less. We don't have to reach the unknown. We can simplify back down to the best and most fulfilling parts of the life we already have.

We don't try to get more. We give up grasping. We let go, relax. Our natural happiness inside is released.

We don't strive for more "effective habits." We drop habits that don't work for us. We stop spending time on anything that doesn't bring us happiness and fulfillment, that isn't necessary for our living or the happiness of the people we care about.

We don't have to say "yes" when people ask us to do things. We just ask ourselves, "Is this something I really want to do, is it part of the life I want?" If the task doesn't connect in some way with our purpose, we say "no." We do less. We enjoy more.

We take items off our lists. Less work. Less shopping. Clear closet clutter. Give away things we don't need. Recycle them. Give up feeling angry or depressed. Close off an old grudge. Forgive our enemies or, harder, our friends!

Stop comparing ourselves to others. Be content with being happy. Be happy with what we have. Stop striving after things that make us restless and unhappy.

Edit our lives. Cut out unsatisfying meetings, travel, relationships. If something's not going anywhere, stop.

Modern life may advocate expensive, difficult training to cope with difficulties. A shrink, guru, or motivation expert supposedly trains us to deal better with stress and our bad behavior. This is like learning all about snakes to deal with them better.

Why bother? Rather, give up or avoid our "snake pits," areas of life where we cope badly. Less is more — dump the stressful and unrewarding parts of our lives. There is always a way, if we are determined.

I have a home in Spain. I go there every few months, to escape business commitments, to focus on thinking and writing. I limit my information inflow:

- ❏ No radio or TV.

- ❏ Few phone calls — a secret number, one phone, no backup, no mobile. Happily, the phone system often fails.

- ❏ See only the few friends I really want to see.

- ❏ Read the newspaper only on Saturday.

Result? I write three or four times faster, and I think much better, than when I'm elsewhere. I love my simple life in Spain. I enjoy every hour — writing, daily cycle ride through the mountains, tennis, dinner with friends. Simple life. Sweet rituals each day. Very cheap.

Think about what's simple, economical, and makes you happy. Read the ideas to simplify your life and look at Jane's pleasure chart opposite.

How about fewer expensive pleasures and more simple ones? Draw your own pleasure chart on the blank one provided on page 138.

| A SIMPLE LIFE MEANS LESS... | AND MORE... |
|---|---|
| work you don't like and aren't good at | work you like and are good at |
| things done for duty | fun and recreation |
| routine | surprises |
| activities with a low return on your energy | activities with a high return on your energy |
| time waiting or worrying | events you enjoy |
| seeing people you don't like | seeing good friends |
| places you don't like | places you like |
| phone calls | time to think |
| travel and commuting | peace and quiet |
| driving | walking and cycling |
| exercise you don't like | exercise you like |
| crises | thinking to avoid crises |
| taking the rough with the smooth | taking the smooth with the smooth |
| information overload | information on your special interests |
| spending | giving away, recycling |
| habits you don't enjoy much | daily rituals you love |
| big things that make little difference | little things that make a big difference |

## Ideas to simplify your life

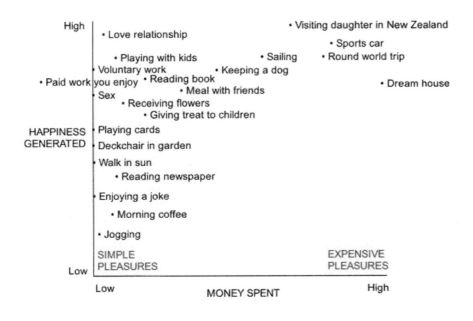

Figure 15  Jane's pleasure chart

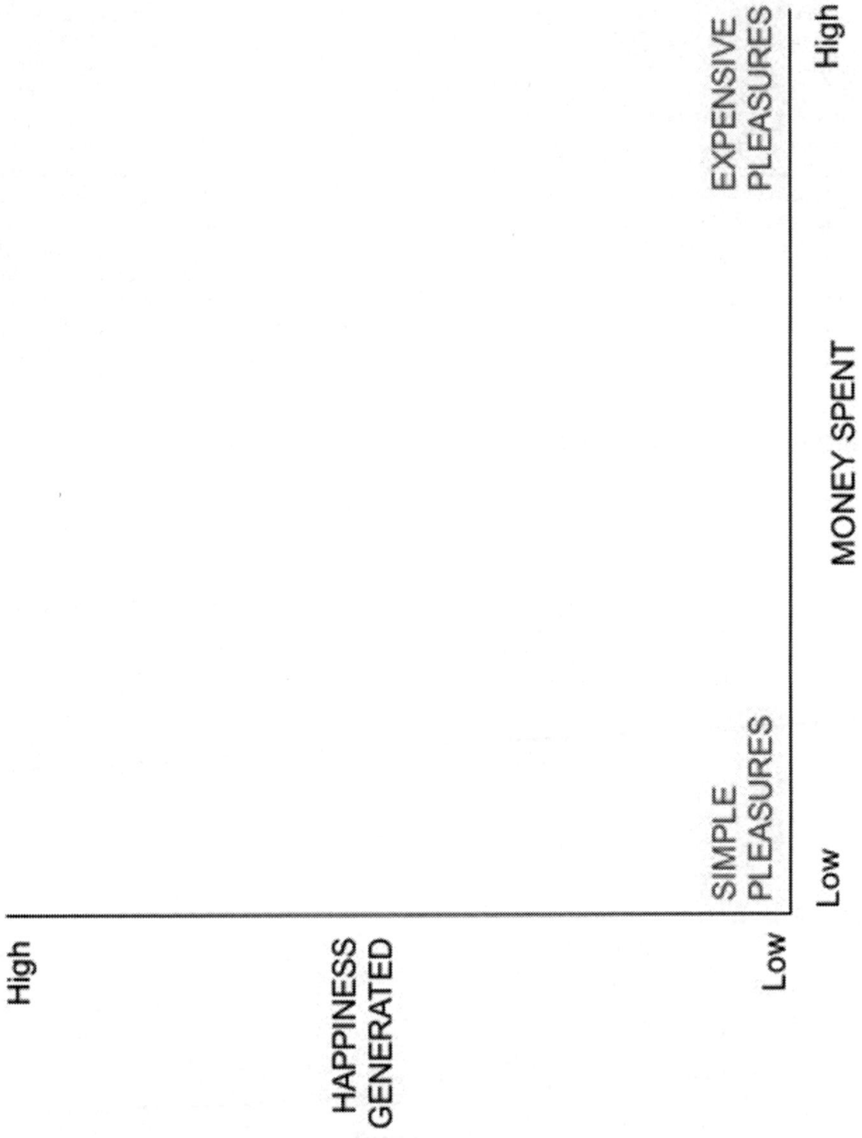

Figure 16  Your pleasure chart

# The 80/20 Way to the simple, good life

## Step 1: Focus on your 80/20 destination

What is the ideal simple, good life for you?

How would your life be simpler? How would your ideal simple life be different?

## Step 2: Find the 80/20 route

The challenge is to find something that is both better and simpler, offering more with less. To simplify, eliminate the things in your life that cause worry or unnecessary aggravation, and give very little benefit relative to the energy or time you expend on them. Eliminate the worry of too much choice or too many ambitions — it's just as possible to be overfocused as underfocused on goals and destinations.

*Avoid your snake pits*

---

**What are your personal snake pits?**




**What could you do to avoid them, or avoid spending so much time in them?**

---

## The 50/5 Way: Getting rid of things that don't matter

Having rid ourselves of negative things, let's dump the many things in life that absorb our energy but give almost nothing back.

The 80/20 Way has a close companion — the 50/5 Way. 50 percent of what we do usually leads to a trivial amount (5 percent) of happiness and results.

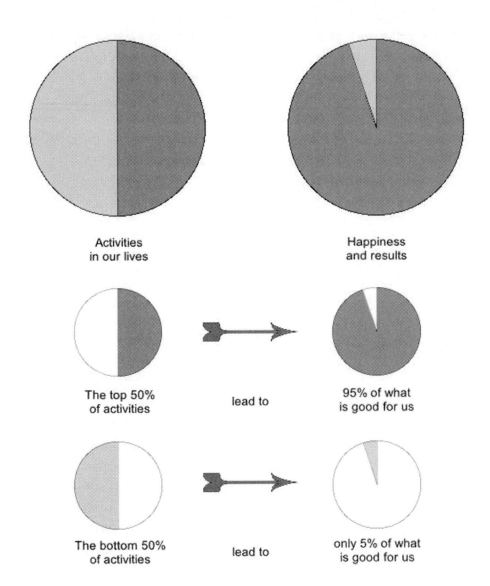

Activities
in our lives

Happiness
and results

The top 50%
of activities

lead to

95% of what
is good for us

The bottom 50%
of activities

lead to

only 5% of what
is good for us

Figure 17  The 50/5 Way

Which tasks clutter your life, yielding little happiness or results?

How can you chop them?

Which simple, inexpensive luxuries could you substitute for expensive luxuries?

| More of these simple luxuries | Fewer of these expensive luxuries |
|---|---|
| | |

How are you going to do this?

Could you imagine a life where most days were full of your favorite simple luxuries?

How can you move toward this ideal life?

## Step 3: Take 80/20 action

What are the three immediate, simple action steps toward your destination — the steps that will take you further toward the simple, good life with the least energy?

Action 1:

Action 2:

Action 3:

Are you going to start today or this week?

When these steps are completed, take another three steps... until you reach *la dolce vita*, a life that challenges and stretches you in the way *you* want, free from worry and the tyranny of more with more. When we realize that less is more and focus on the few things that matter, it's *always* possible to find more with less — a professional and personal life that is simple, refreshing, and constructed around what each of us loves doing.

# PART III

# Making It Happen

# The Power of Parsimonious Positive Action

If to do were as easy as to know what were good to do, chapels would be churches and poor men's cottages princes' palaces.

William Shakespeare, *The Merchant of Venice*

Two identical twins, Julie and Sandra, are very shy. A great mutual friend is giving a party they really want to attend, so they decide to cure their shyness. They turn to the self-help section of their local bookstore.

Julie buys a bestseller about positive thinking by a famous motivational coach. She learns that she must suppress her shyness. Whenever she feels shy, *bing*, she should dismiss the thought. She should tell herself that she isn't shy any more, that inside her introvert personality there is an extrovert that can be liberated.

On the afternoon of the party, Julie is having second thoughts. She is thinking, "I always feel awkward at parties, let's not go." But she tries to stimulate some positive thinking. She says to herself, "Nonsense, my girl! You can be the life and soul of the party! Let's pretend you're not shy at all and you won't be."

Just before leaving, to calm her nerves and help awaken the extrovert within, she has a large vodka and tonic.

In the taxi with Sandra, Julie feels all pumped up. Positive thinking is working! But when they arrive at the party, she senses the vodka wearing off, the bar is crowded, and she is anxious as usual. She tries to feel positive, but after 15 minutes she hasn't talked to anyone, not even Sandra, who's deep in conversation with a gorgeous young man. Not wishing to interrupt and feeling as bad as ever, Julie leaves after half an hour. The only answer is: no more parties! Perhaps she can meet a man at work.

At breakfast, Julie asks Sandra how she got on.

"Great!" says Sandra, noticing Julie's depressed face too late.

"How," Julie asks, "did you manage to suppress your shyness?"

"The thing is, I didn't. When you were all bubbly in the taxi, I was as anxious as ever and dreading the party. But the book I bought told me not to worry about feeling timid, just to take some positive action. So I said to myself, 'However bad you feel, Sandra, you are going to go up to the first man you like and introduce yourself and say something, anything. You are going to do this within 10 minutes of arriving. If the first man isn't friendly, that's OK, try two other men and if that doesn't work, you don't have to worry about talking to anyone else — at least you've tried.' So I saw this cute guy with the blue shirt and asked him to dance. I was watching carefully and I think he half-smiled at me. Anyway, he said yes, and introduced me to his friends. After two dances, I wasn't nervous any more."

"What was the book?"

"Oh, I've got it upstairs, some funny title with numbers in it."

Positive thinking may work for the small minority of people who are natural optimists — but they don't need help. The problem with positive thinking — and with much advice from self-help gurus — is that it can be unrealistic and lead us to deny our emotions. Kidding ourselves that black is white does not usually work for long.

We cannot change how we feel about life very easily or quickly, nor do we need to. All of us are bound to continue having "negative" emotions: feeling down, anxious, angry, or weak. These emotions are valuable, because they tell us something useful about ourselves.

Emotions should be accepted, not crushed. We should use our deliberate, thinking capacity to "talk to" our emotions and reason with them. Treat emotions like people with whom we disagree. Instead of interrupting them, "have a cup of tea" with them, let them have their say, admit your feelings — and yet resolve to act positively.

Julie attempted to quash her shyness, but it simply popped up again at the party, causing her spirits to sag. Sandra did not beat down her shyness, so she was not depressed when she felt shy. She accepted that she was shy and might well come back from the party feeling bad, but she decided to take a few actions that had the result she wanted. When she took action, she was shy and admitted it to herself. Yet she forced herself to act — and before long her action had changed everything, including her feelings.

In the Nazi death camps, the writer and therapist Viktor Frankl knew that his chances of survival were slim. He even calculated the odds — twenty-eight to one against. There was no power in the power of positive thinking at Auschwitz — being unrealistic led straight to the gas oven.

Yet Frankl acted positively. "When I was taken to Auschwitz," he wrote, "a manuscript of mine ready for publication was confiscated... when in a camp in Bavaria I fell ill with typhus fever, I jotted down on little scraps of paper many notes intended to enable me to rewrite the manuscript, should I live to the day of liberation. I am sure that this reconstruction of my lost manuscript in the dark barracks of a Bavarian concentration camp assisted me in overcoming the danger of cardiovascular collapse."

Frankl also composed speeches in his head and imagined himself giving them to audiences after the war, so that the death camps could never recur. Though he thought it extremely unlikely that he would survive, he stopped worrying and took all the positive action he could.

His reconstructed book, *Man's Search for Meaning*, sold over nine million copies. The Library of Congress voted it one of the ten most influential books of the twentieth century.[1]

**V**iktor Frankl didn't deny his emotions. His book is bleak and realistic about the horrors of camp life. Still, he asked himself, "What can I do that might possibly work, that will give me a reason to continue living?" And then he acted — even though most of the time he felt depressed, hungry, and physically tormented. He didn't attempt to *think* positively, just to *act* positively.

He noted that other individuals also managed to act positively: "The experiences of camp life show man does have a choice of action... We who lived in concentration camps can remember the men who walked through the huts comforting others, giving away their last piece of bread."

## If inmates of a concentration camp

## can take positive action,

### can't we *all?*

Next time you feel blue, ask what positive action you can try to change your mood. If you're stumped, try one — or all — of these:

❑ Stand upright, stretch, and smile at yourself in the mirror; then find another person to smile at — even if it's a stranger!

❑ Go for a long walk or take some other exercise.

❑ Perform an act of kindness.

However bad our circumstances or emotions, we can change our lives by a few 80/20 actions — the relatively easy actions that make such a big difference to our happiness and the happiness of people around us.

The Shakespeare quote at the beginning of the chapter is right: it's a lot more difficult to act than to know what to do. How many times have we all resolved to do something positive, only to resume our normal lives without making that decisive step? To change our lives, we have to make things *easier* on ourselves — we have to achieve decisive change, but do it without superhuman effort. This is where the 80/20 Way is so different and so much more effective, for two reasons.

One, the 80/20 Way does not require us to change how we *feel*. That will come later, naturally, without strain, as our actions produce the desired results.

Two, we don't have to increase the effort and energy we already bring to our daily lives. By focusing on less is more — the very few things that really matter to us — we can transform our life while actually exerting less effort and having fewer worries than now. If we are highly selective about what we want and limit ourselves to the key things that express our individuality, we can be lazier and yet act more effectively. By using the idea of more with less, we can find a much better solution that uses less energy.

The secret of 80/20 action is to be parsimonious[2] in our *positive actions*. Be stingy and economical with your energy. There's a limited amount of it. Only use it in those few actions that can really make you happy and powerful.

It's easier to change a few of the things we *do* than the things we habitually *think* and *feel*. Take the few right *actions* and your feelings will take care of themselves.

All you have to do is reflect, then act:

- ❏  Work out what you want: the few things that are most important to you. This is the 80/20 *destination*.

- ❏  Work out the easiest route for you: the few actions that will produce the results you want with the least strain and stress. This is the 80/20 *route*.

- ❏  Take the few most important next steps along the route. This is 80/20 *action*.

So far in this book, we've concentrated on the thinking. Now is the time to experience less is more and more with less — the time to *act*.

The good news is that we can apply the 80/20 Way to the process of 80/20 action. There's a simple action program that really does work. And here it is, in our final chapter...

# Your 80/20 Happiness Plan

Just Do It

Nike slogan

There is a true story about a troop of young Hungarian soldiers lost in the Alps during training. In abysmal weather, with no food or supplies, they were cut off from their colleagues. After two days of snow and sleet, they were frozen and weak from hunger. They had no idea how to get back to base. They lost the will to live.

Then a miracle happened. Searching for a cigarette in the lining of his tunic, one of the soldiers suddenly found an old map. The soldiers confidently used the map to march through the mountains back to safety.

It was only when they were warm and fed at base camp that they discovered it was a map of the Pyrenees, some 2,000 kilometers away.

This story has two valuable lessons:

❏ It is better to act constructively than to have the right answer and not act.

❏ Each of us has to find our own answer, or adapt someone else's answer to our own circumstances. The soldiers got home safely because they made sense of the map for themselves and related it to their immediate surroundings.

Now is the time for you to act, to adapt the insights from the 80/20 Way to suit your own desires, inclinations, and needs. You can make your life very much better, without fuss, bother, or superhuman effort.

But this does require *action*:

❏     Set aside a regular time and day to spend an hour a week on your 80/20 happiness plan — for example, 4 pm Sunday. Any time slot will do, but stick to it.

❏     Ideally, get a friend to be your mutual mentor — another reader of *Living the 80/20 Way* who wants to change their life. Compare notes on your progress, perhaps meeting for your weekly 80/20 happiness plan hour.

❏     Complete your 80/20 happiness plan. This is easy, a summary of what you've already decided and written down in Part II. Figure 18 gives an example and Figure 19 is blank for you to complete.[1]

## *Hints for completing your 80/20 happiness plan*

1     Refer back to the notes you made in Chapters 4–8.

2     Make your 80/20 destination very specific. Once you have arrived at the destination, choose another specific one.

3     Select the 80/20 route(s) that you will enjoy and that will take you to your destination. Choose a route that offers more with less: that is both more rewarding and easier than what you would normally do. You must believe that you are capable of traveling the route successfully; if not, pick an easier route.

4     Always write down one, two, or three 80/20 happiness actions. List them in the order you will take them.

5    Pick one of the five areas (your self; work and success; money; relationships; the simple, good life) to start with. The area to pick is the one uppermost in your mind at the moment — where you most want things to improve — or the area where it will be easiest for you to act successfully. "Sequence" means the order in which you will tackle all five areas — you can review the sequence later, after success in the first area.

6    "Date to start action" should be a particular week, month, or year. Write in the actual date (e.g. January 2005).

7    Finish one 80/20 action before you move on to another.

8    If any 80/20 route or action is not working, choose another. But give it a chance before you switch.

Use your weekly 80/20 happiness plan hour to track progress, using your 80/20 happiness plan progress chart. Caroline's chart (Figure 20) gives you the idea, and Figures 21–32 are progress charts to last you 12 months.

Caroline has decided to attack the *money* area first. The left side of Figure 20 comes straight from the money section of Figure 18. The right side lists the weeks.

Caroline enters her first 80/20 action. She completes it the first week. She then inserts the second 80/20 action, noting her headway each week. By week 4 she has found a Christmas vacation job. Having taken care of the money area, she advances the following week to the work and success area.

## *Hints for completing your 80/20 happiness plan progress chart*

❑    Under "area," put the one you've chosen to tackle first. On the left-hand side, repeat what you've written under that area in Figure 19.

❑   On the right, enter the dates for the week ends this month, then write the first 80/20 action. Note your progress on the right at the end of each week.

❑   When the first 80/20 action is completed, enter the second 80/20 action, and so on.

❑   If all 80/20 actions are achieved within the month, celebrate – take the rest of the month off. Next month, move on to the second area.

On the way to and from work each day, remind yourself of your 80/20 action. Write it in your diary or on postcard-size index cards placed in your purse or wallet. Even better, make the 80/20 action so simple and clear that you remember it all the time. Visualize yourself taking your 80/20 action to help make it reality.

Don't set deadlines for your 80/20 actions. Deadlines turn out either too easy or, more often, too hard. As long as you're making headway, continue your 80/20 action until it's done.

Some 80/20 actions will take a day; others may take several months or years. If you don't feel that you are moving along nicely, choose another action or route and start again. Be your own judge of progress – you're the beneficiary!

| CHAPTER | 5 | 6 | 7 | 8 | 9 |
|---|---|---|---|---|---|
| AREA | YOUR SELF | WORK AND SUCCESS | MONEY | RELATIONSHIPS | SIMPLE, GOOD LIFE |
| 80/20 DESTINATION | Become expert on care for stray dogs | Find job I really enjoy | Afford deposit on own home by 2007 | Find lover who is secure, optimistic, loving, and likes dogs | Ideal life is spending all time with animals and animal lovers |
| 80/20 ROUTE(S) | Find three mentors who are experts already | Train as vet | Save and invest 10% of income automatically Take evening and weekend jobs | Meet men at animal rescue shelter and vet school | Persuade parents to let me finish school and go to vet college |
| 80/20 ACTION | 1 Identify best mentors 2 Work out how I can help them 3 Approach them | 1 Pass biology exams 2 Visit vet colleges 3 Get accepted at chosen college | 1 Open savings account and have 10% of income deducted automatically 2 Find job for vacation | 1 Volunteer at shelter 2 Get to know Sean and Peter much better | 1 Get top grade in biology 2 Get Uncle Tom to persuade parents |
| SEQUENCE | 5 | 2 | 1 | 4 | 3 |
| ACTION START DATE | Later | This year | This week/month | Next year | This year |

Figure 18  Caroline's 80/20 happiness plan

| CHAPTER | | 5 | 6 | 7 | 8 | 9 | | |
|---|---|---|---|---|---|---|---|---|
| AREA | | YOUR SELF | WORK AND SUCCESS | MONEY | RELATIONSHIPS | SIMPLE, GOOD LIFE | | |
| 80/20 DESTINATION | | | | | | | | |
| 80/20 ROUTE(S) | | | | | | | | |
| 80/20 ACTION | | | | | | | | |
| SEQUENCE | | | | | | | | |
| ACTION START DATE | | | | | | | | |

Figure 19  Your 80/20 happiness plan

MONTH:    YEAR:

| WEEK ENDING | 80/20 ACTION | PROGRESS |
|---|---|---|
| 8 Nov | 1 Open savings account etc. | Completed |
| 15 Nov | 2 Find job for vacation | Completed list of 7 firms |
| 22 Nov | ditto | Applied in person to 5 of them |
| 29 Nov | ditto | Accepted for Christmas job — completed |

THE 80/20 WAY

| AREA | Money |
|---|---|
| 80/20 DESTINATION | Afford deposit on own home by 2007 |
| 80/20 ROUTE(S) | Save and invest 10% of income automatically. Take evening and weekend jobs |
| 80/20 ACTION 1 | Open savings account and have 10% of income deducted automatically |
| 2 | Find job for vacation |
| 3 | |

Figure 20  Caroline's 80/20 happiness plan progress chart

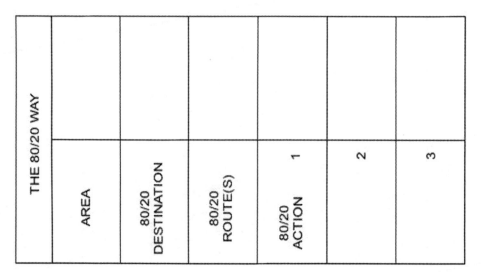

| YEAR: | | | | | | |
|---|---|---|---|---|---|---|
| | PROGRESS | | | | | |
| | 80/20 ACTION | | | | | |
| MONTH: | WEEK ENDING | | | | | |

| THE 80/20 WAY | | | | | | |
|---|---|---|---|---|---|---|
| | AREA | | | | | |
| | 80/20 DESTINATION | | | | | |
| | 80/20 ROUTE(S) | | | | | |
| | 80/20 ACTION | 1 | 2 | 3 | | |

Figure 21  Your 80/20 happiness plan progress chart

Worksheet may be copied for personal use only, not for commercial purposes.

| MONTH: | | | | | | YEAR: |
|---|---|---|---|---|---|---|
| WEEK ENDING | 80/20 ACTION | PROGRESS | | | | |
| | | | | | | |
| | | | | | | |
| | | | | | | |
| | | | | | | |

| THE 80/20 WAY | | | | | |
|---|---|---|---|---|---|
| AREA | 80/20 DESTINATION | 80/20 ROUTE(S) | 80/20 ACTION | | |
| | | | 1 | | |
| | | | 2 | | |
| | | | 3 | | |

Figure 22 Your 80/20 happiness plan progress chart

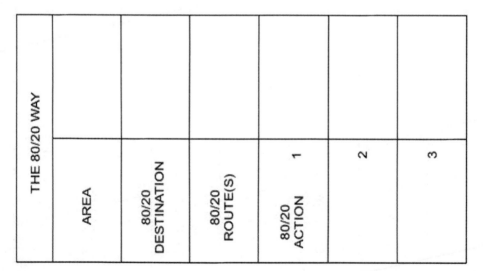

| MONTH: | | | | YEAR: | |
|---|---|---|---|---|---|
| WEEK ENDING | 80/20 ACTION | PROGRESS | | | |
| | | | | | |
| | | | | | |
| | | | | | |

| THE 80/20 WAY | | | | | |
|---|---|---|---|---|---|
| | | | | | |
| AREA | 80/20 DESTINATION | 80/20 ROUTE(S) | 80/20 ACTION | | |
| | | | 1 | 2 | 3 |

Figure 23  Your 80/20 happiness plan progress chart

Worksheet may be copied for personal use only, not for commercial purposes.

| MONTH: | | | | | YEAR: |
|---|---|---|---|---|---|
| WEEK ENDING | 80/20 ACTION | PROGRESS | | | |
| | | | | | |
| | | | | | |
| | | | | | |
| | | | | | |

| THE 80/20 WAY | | | | | |
|---|---|---|---|---|---|
| AREA | 80/20 DESTINATION | 80/20 ROUTE(S) | 80/20 ACTION | | |
| | | | 1 | | |
| | | | 2 | | |
| | | | 3 | | |

Figure 24  Your 80/20 happiness plan progress chart

Worksheet may be copied for personal use only, not for commercial purposes.

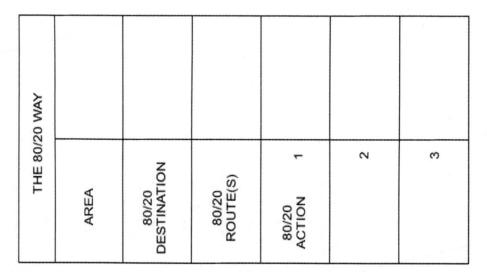

| YEAR: | | | | | | |
|---|---|---|---|---|---|---|
| | PROGRESS | | | | | |
| | 80/20 ACTION | | | | | |
| MONTH: | WEEK ENDING | | | | | |

| THE 80/20 WAY | | | | | | |
|---|---|---|---|---|---|---|
| | AREA | | | | | |
| | 80/20 DESTINATION | | | | | |
| | 80/20 ROUTE(S) | | | | | |
| | 80/20 ACTION | 1 | 2 | 3 | | |

Figure 25 Your 80/20 happiness plan progress chart

| MONTH: | | | | YEAR: | | |
|---|---|---|---|---|---|---|
| WEEK ENDING | 80/20 ACTION | PROGRESS | | | | |
| | | | | | | |
| | | | | | | |

| THE 80/20 WAY | | | | | | |
|---|---|---|---|---|---|---|
| AREA | 80/20 DESTINATION | 80/20 ROUTE(S) | 80/20 ACTION | 1 | 2 | 3 |
| | | | | | | |

Figure 26  Your 80/20 happiness plan progress chart

| MONTH: | | | | YEAR: | | |
|---|---|---|---|---|---|---|
| WEEK ENDING | 80/20 ACTION | PROGRESS | | | | |
| | | | | | | |
| | | | | | | |
| | | | | | | |
| | | | | | | |

| THE 80/20 WAY | | | | | | |
|---|---|---|---|---|---|---|
| | | | | | | |
| AREA | 80/20 DESTINATION | 80/20 ROUTE(S) | 80/20 ACTION 1 | 2 | 3 | |

Figure 27  Your 80/20 happiness plan progress chart

| MONTH: | | | | YEAR: | |
|---|---|---|---|---|---|
| WEEK ENDING | 80/20 ACTION | PROGRESS | | | |
| | | | | | |
| | | | | | |
| | | | | | |

| THE 80/20 WAY | | | | | |
|---|---|---|---|---|---|
| AREA | 80/20 DESTINATION | 80/20 ROUTE(S) | 80/20 ACTION | | |
| | | | 1 | 2 | 3 |

Figure 28  Your 80/20 happiness plan progress chart

Worksheet may be copied for personal use only, not for commercial purposes.

| MONTH: | | | YEAR: | | |
|---|---|---|---|---|---|
| WEEK ENDING | 80/20 ACTION | PROGRESS | | | |
| | | | | | |
| | | | | | |
| | | | | | |
| | | | | | |

| THE 80/20 WAY | | | | | |
|---|---|---|---|---|---|
| AREA | 80/20 DESTINATION | 80/20 ROUTE(S) | 80/20 ACTION | | |
| | | | 1 | | |
| | | | 2 | | |
| | | | 3 | | |

Figure 29  Your 80/20 happiness plan progress chart

Worksheet may be copied for personal use only, not for commercial purposes.

| MONTH: | | | | YEAR: | |
|--------|--|--|--|-------|--|
| WEEK ENDING | 80/20 ACTION | PROGRESS | | | |
| | | | | | |
| | | | | | |
| | | | | | |
| | | | | | |

| THE 80/20 WAY | | | | | |
|---------------|--|--|--|--|--|
| AREA | 80/20 DESTINATION | 80/20 ROUTE(S) | 80/20 ACTION | | |
| | | | 1 | 2 | 3 |
| | | | | | |

Figure 30  Your 80/20 happiness plan progress chart

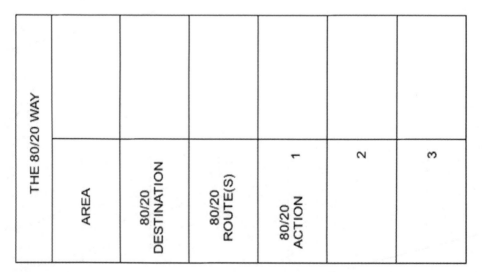

Figure 31 Your 80/20 happiness plan progress chart

| YEAR: | | | | | | |
|---|---|---|---|---|---|---|
| MONTH: | PROGRESS | | | | | |
| | 80/20 ACTION | | | | | |
| | WEEK ENDING | | | | | |

| THE 80/20 WAY | | | | | | |
|---|---|---|---|---|---|---|
| | AREA | | | | | |
| | 80/20 DESTINATION | | | | | |
| | 80/20 ROUTE(S) | | | | | |
| | 80/20 ACTION | 1 | 2 | 3 | | |

Figure 32 Your 80/20 happiness plan progress chart

## Farewell

In Lewis Carroll's *Through the Looking Glass*, the Red Queen drags Alice into a mad dash:

> they were running hand in hand, and the Queen went so fast that it was all she could do to keep up with her: and still the Queen kept crying, "Faster! Faster!", but Alice felt she *could not* go faster, though she had no breath to say so.
>
> The most curious part of the thing was, that the trees and the other things round them never changed their places at all: however fast they went, they never seemed to pass anything...
>
> "Now! Now!" cried the Queen. "Faster! Faster!" And they went so fast that at last they seemed to skim through the air, hardly touching the ground with their feet, till suddenly, just as Alice was getting quite exhausted, they stopped, and she found herself sitting on the ground, breathless and giddy...
>
> Alice looked round her in great surprise. "Why, I do believe we've been under this tree the whole time! Everything's just as it was!"
>
> "Of course it is," said the Queen. "What would you have it?"
>
> "Well, in our country," said Alice, still panting a little, "you'd generally get to somewhere else — if you ran very fast for a long time as we've being doing."
>
> "A slow sort of country!" said the Queen. "Now, *here*, you see, it takes all the running you can do, to keep in the same place. If you want to get somewhere else, you must run at least twice as fast as that!"[2]

Lewis Carroll could have been satirizing today's fast-track world, which urges us to go faster and seek more with more. But as Alice found, when we speed up we exhaust ourselves without getting anywhere. The tread-mill of modern life relentlessly cranks up, we run faster and faster, but never arrive at happiness. Like running at the gym, we sweat, we get tired, yet we stay where we were.

The fast track bestows only the illusion of speed. Like a theme park rollercoaster, it's scary and thrilling, yet it takes us nowhere.

If speeding up takes us nowhere, slowing down can take us everywhere. Contrary to common opinion, less is more. Only by concentrating on the few important and vital things, and refusing to worry over the mass of triv-ial ones, can we find happiness. Only by doing less can we live more. Only by insisting on more with less can we fulfill our individual destiny.

We have seen that more with less is the principle behind marvelous achievements in business, economics, science, and technology. The watchwords of success are focus, selectivity, and innovation.

The 80/20 Way translates the same principle to our individual lives. We don't have to accept the current fad — surely one that will seem bizarre and ridiculous to observers a few decades ahead — for more with more. More with more is stupid. It wastes human potential. It insults human intelligence and ingenuity. It flunks any objective test of social progress. More with more is just a wet dream for misguided yuppies.

To find meaning in life, we have to reach inside ourselves: define the few things that we care about, the things we want to love and devote our-selves to, the things we are good at and enjoy. Having found these things, everything else is trivial. Fulfilled and happy creating more with less, we can safely ignore the shrill fad for more with more and "Faster! Faster!".

# But the 80/20 Way still requires *effort...*

In this book I've suggested a more intelligent and worry-free path through life, an easier way to achievement and self-realization. More with less is much easier than more with more.

Yet in one respect, the 80/20 Way is harder. *It is harder to start.* Because all the assumptions of the modern world push us toward more is more and more with more, we need self-confidence and resolve to leave the crowd.

To reject more with more in favor of more with less requires less labor and yields greater happiness and fulfillment, yet also demands a degree of intellectual courage. We have to reject the modern treadmill and stop doing what other ambitious people are doing. We must get rid of more is more and more with more. We have to work out where less can be more and stick to our guns when friends and colleagues think we're nuts.

I dare to guess that you now believe in less is more and more with less. But reading this book has been useless unless you start *behaving* differently.

Albert Einstein said that every problem should be made as simple as possible, but not simpler. The 80/20 Way makes everything as easy as possible, but not easier. Ultimately, to make a life — to take action that will lead to the best life you can make — requires some new and different effort. Otherwise, we would be robots and life wouldn't be worth crafting.

Nevertheless, effort is effortless when driven by desire and love. Too often we're driven not by desire, not by what we love, but by the dead hand of guilt, worry, or duty. Duty, John Fowles wrote, "largely consists of pretending that the trivial is critical." Duty wastes life energy. All great human accomplishments have been driven not by duty but by passion.

Our lives are most enjoyable and valuable when we are driven by the few things that excite us. If we are not excited, nothing is of any use. If we are not ourselves, little will come of our lives. If we are excited and ourselves, however, there is no limit to our happiness or achievement.

The vision behind the 80/20 Way is a world where we are all individuals, responsible for ourselves, discovering and enjoying our unique place in the universe, leaving behind fond memories, happy children, or some enhancement of art, science, literature, or service to other people.

It is awesome to realize that most of life is trivial and most of what we do is unworthy of us. Of course, we shouldn't look down on the mundane tasks of life: the cleaning, the washing-up, the need to make a living. What matters is how and why we do what we do. Anything that gives meaning to our life or happiness is precious. But to drift aimlessly through life, without being happy or making other people happy, without realizing the best of what we could become — what a waste!

Yes, it takes a little effort to get on the 80/20 Way — you don't need 20/20 vision, but you do need 80/20 vision. Yes, it requires a different attitude. Yes, you must stand out from the crowd. Yes, you must cast off the sticky chains of modern convention. Yes, it takes action. But you *can* do it. Decide now that you *will*. Start to do it! Once you get the hang of it, it will seem the easiest way of all.

Without action, you may have enjoyed this book, but that pleasure will soon fade. My warm wish is that you take the few, small but well-directed actions that will transform your life, enabling your happiness to overflow and flood the people around you, the ones you love. To multiply happiness, start those few actions right away.

# Notes

## Chapter 1

1 Data from the census on April 21, 1991 relating to England alone (not including the rest of the United Kingdom) from the website www.citypopulation.de.
2 *The Economist*, 27 November 1993, p. 33.
3 *The Economist*, 17 July 1993, p. 61.
4 Stanley Milgram (1967) "The small-world problem," *Psychology Today*, Vol. 2, pp. 60–67.
5 Malcolm Gladwell (2000) *The Tipping Point: How Little Things Can Make a Big Difference*, Boston: Little, Brown.

## Chapter 2

1 I am grateful to the late, greatly missed Douglas Adams for these examples. See Douglas Adams (2002) *The Salmon of Doubt: Hitchhiking the Galaxy One Last Time*, New York: Harmony.
2 If you value them.
3 This means no cell phone, pager, email, or other distractions, especially not work-related ones.

## Chapter 3

1 Theodore Zeldin (1995) *An Intimate History of Humanity*, New York: HarperCollins.

## Chapter 4

1 Using contraception, for example; whether right or wrong, it is opposed to our genes' interests.

## Chapter 6

1 See Martin E P Seligman (2003) *Authentic Happiness: Using the New Positive Psychology to Realize Your Potential for Deep Fulfillment*, London: Nicholas Brealey.
2 Joe Dominguez and Vicki Robin (1992) *Your Money or Your Life: Transforming Your Relationship with Money and Achieving Financial Independence*, New York: Viking Penguin. A brilliant free 25-page summary of the book by Clare Moss and Laurence Toltz is available at www.simpleliving.net/ymoyl/fom-about-summary.asp or see the website www.simpleliving.net.

## Chapter 7

1 If in doubt, consult Seligman, *op cit*, pp 189–95.
2 See Martin E P Seligman (1991) *Learned Optimism*, New York: Knopf.

## Chapter 9

1 Viktor E Frankl (1946, 1984) *Man's Search for Meaning*, New York: Washington Square Press.
2 By "parsimonious" I mean being economical and therefore highly selective with our actions.

## *Chapter 10*

1 The worksheets may be copied for personal use only, not for commercial purposes.
2 Lewis Carroll (1872) *Through the Looking Glass, and What Alice Found There*, London: Macmillan. See Penguin Classics edition of Lewis Carroll (1998) *Alice's Adventures in Wonderland* and *Through the Looking Glass*, London: Penguin, pp. 141–3.

# *Index*

# *Acknowledgments*

The idea for a simple, self-help book based on the 80/20 principle came, independently, from Laurence Toltz and Nicholas Brealey. Steve Gersowsky was also instrumental in encouraging me to write a book that would be accessible to everyone.

I owe a huge debt to Laurence Toltz for his critique and encouragement every step of the way. He has been extraordinarily generous with his time and many of his ideas are incorporated here. His only motivation has been to help readers live a fuller and better life without getting hooked on the materialistic drug of "more" that is so prevalent and destructive today. Laurence himself is an author, so please look out for his excellent books.

I have also received invaluable views, feedback, and critiques along the way from Tom Butler-Bowden, whose inclusion of *The 80/20 Principle* in his terrific book *50 Self-Help Classics* also spurred me to write a sequel.

The other person who has influenced me greatly is Jonathan Yudelowitz, a psychologist and business coach. Jon and I were originally going to write this book together and pretty much all the psychological ideas here come from his insight. Jon is a world-class coach, specializing in helping CEOs and their teams work together to beat competition.

Drafts of the book — oh, so many drafts, you have no idea how difficult it is to write a short, simple book — were scrutinized and found wanting by many of my friends and I'm grateful to them all. I'd particularly like to mention Andy Costain, Mary Saxe-Falstein, Juliet Johnson, Penelope Toltz, Robin Field, Chris Eyles, Matthew Grimsdale, Anthony Rice, and Jamie Reeve. Special thanks also especially to my friend and personal assistant Aaron Calder, who has helped with the book in innumerable important ways.

My toughest critic has been Nicholas Brealey and a better book has been forged in the fire of his feedback. A bouquet also to Angie Tainsh and Victoria Bullock for their excellent work on the conception and marketing of the book, and special thanks to Sally Lansdell for her superb editing, figure design, and encyclopedic knowledge of transportation in Bedrock.

Finally, thanks to the huge number of readers of my earlier books, especially those of *The 80/20 Principle*, who have shared with me how the books have helped their lives. The pointers from that experience have been included here so that many new readers can benefit. If you have any comments on *Living the 80/20 Way*, please email them to richardjohnkoch@aol.com.

Visit the 80/20 website

www.the8020principle.com


The site provides:

A structured link to 80/20 material on the web

A market space to exchange services and
products related to the 80/20 principle

A forum for 80/20 ideas


Visit the site today!

# THE 80/20 PRINCIPLE
## The Secret of Achieving More with Less

## RICHARD KOCH

The 80/20 Principle – that 80 percent of results flow from just 20 percent of causes – is the one true principle of highly effective people and organizations. In one of the decade's most original, provocative and powerful books, *The 80/20 Principle* shows how you can achieve much more with much less effort, time and resources, simply by concentrating on the all-important 20 percent.

Astonishingly, though the 80/20 Principle has greatly influenced today's world, this is the first book that shows how to use it in a systematic and practical way.

In *The 80/20 Principle*, Richard Koch drives home the truth and power of the principle through a wide range of examples from business, personal and social spheres. Generally, 20 percent of products account for 80 percent of sales value and profits; so do 20 percent of customers; 20 percent of criminals account for 80 percent of the loot; 20 percent of motorists cause 80 percent of accidents; 20 percent of your carpets get 80 percent of the wear; and 20 percent of your clothes are worn 80 percent of the time.

The 80/20 Principle is the key to controlling our lives. Most of what we do has trivial results. A little of what we do really matters. So if we focus on the latter, we can control events instead of being controlled by them, and achieve several times the results.

**£12.99**
**Paperback ISBN 1 85788 168 0**
**304pp 234x156mm**

# THE 80/20 INDIVIDUAL
## The Nine Essentials of 80/20 Success at Work

## RICHARD KOCH

In this powerful sequel to his classic bestseller *The 80/20 Principle*, Richard Koch uniquely makes the connection between the rise of the individual and the 80/20 Principle – achieving more with less – to create great new wealth.

From big business to small, from Hollywood to sport, Richard Koch demonstrates how the innovative individual now has the competitive advantage.

*The 80/20 Principle* demonstrated the concept, *The 80/20 Individual* shows how to put it into practice for your own professional success. Here Richard Koch reveals how innovative individuals are taking over the world and how you can join in the revolution – creating new wealth and wellbeing in a twenty-first-century individualism.

The 80/20 Principle enables anyone who is determined, bright or shrewd to stamp their footprint on the world, to become an 80/20 person. 80/20 people cut across all established fields and all walks of life: politics, business, social work and not-for-profits, sports, entertainment and the media.

*The 80/20 Individual* is a new, updated and abridged paperback edition of the bestselling hardback *The 80/20 Revolution*, adapted to be a practical guide for business professionals and entrepreneurs.

**£12.99**
**Paperback ISBN 1 85788 310 1**
**282pp 234x156mm**

NICHOLAS BREALEY PUBLISHING

# new *books* **new** *business*

## ORDER FORM

| Title | Price | Qty | Cost |
|---|---|---|---|
| The 80/20 Principle | | | |
| The 80/20 Individual | | | |
| Postage UK or surface mail outside the UK (replace with £8.00 for airmail) | | | +£2.95 |
| TOTAL | | | |

Titles are available from all good bookshops, OR
SEND YOUR COMPLETED ORDER TO: Nicholas Brealey Publishing
3–5 Spafield St                                                                         PO Box 700
London EC1R 4QB                                          Yarmouth, Maine 04096, USA
Tel: +44 (0)20 7239 0360                                            Tel: (888) BREALEY
Fax: +44 (0)20 7329 0370                                          Fax: (207) 846 5181
BY CHEQUE: I enclose a cheque (payable to Nicholas Brealey Publishing)
for.................

BY CREDIT CARD: I authorize you to debit my credit card account for . . . . .
   My Mastercard/Visa/American Express/Diners Club card number is:

Expiry date: . . . . . . . . . . . . . . . . . . . . . . . . . . . . . . . . . . . . . . . . . . . . .
Tel no:  . . . . . . . . . . . . . . . . . . . . . . . . . . . . . . . . . . . . . . . . . . . . . . . . .
Cardholder's name:  . . . . . . . . . . . . . . . . . . . . . . . . . . . . . . . . . . . . . . .

Signature: . . . . . . . . . . . . . . . . . . . . . . . . . . . . . . . . . . . . . . . . . . . . . . .
Position:  . . . . . . . . . . . . . . . . . . . . . . . . . . . . . . . . . . . . . . . . . . . . . . . .
Organization: . . . . . . . . . . . . . . . . . . . . . . . . . . . . . . . . . . . . . . . . . . . . .
Address:  . . . . . . . . . . . . . . . . . . . . . . . . . . . . . . . . . . . . . . . . . . . . . . . .
. . . . . . . . . . . . . . . . . . . . . . . . . . . . . . . . . . . . . . . . . . . . . . . . . . . . . .
Postcode:  . . . . . . . . . . . . . . . . . . . . . . . . . . . . . . . . . . . . . . . . . . . . . . .